RUSSIA OBSERVED

Advisory Editors

HARMON TUPPER   HARRY W. NERHOOD

DIARY OF GEORGE MIFFLIN DALLAS UNITED STATES MINISTER TO RUSSIA

1837-1839

ARNO PRESS & THE NEW YORK TIMES

New York • 1970

Reprint edition 1970 by Arno Press, Inc.

Library of Congress Catalog Card No. 70-115527
ISBN 0-405-03019-3

Russia Observed
ISBN for complete set 0-405-03000-2

Reprinted from a copy in
the Newark Public Library

Manufactured in the United States of America

DIARY
OF
GEORGE MIFFLIN DALLAS

DIARY

OF

GEORGE MIFFLIN DALLAS

*While United States Minister to Russia
1837 to 1839*

EDITED BY
SUSAN DALLAS

PHILADELPHIA
J. B. LIPPINCOTT COMPANY
1892

COPYRIGHT, 1892,
BY
SUSAN DALLAS.

PRINTED BY J. B. LIPPINCOTT COMPANY, PHILADELPHIA.

PREFATORY.

My dear Miss Dallas:

All lovers of literature, and especially all students of history, will, I am sure, hail with pleasure the publication of your father's diaries of the events of his daily life at the courts of Russia and Great Britain, which are soon to appear under the editorial auspices of his daughter.

His observation of affairs and his experiences, diplomatic and personal, while Envoy Extraordinary and Minister Plenipotentiary at the courts of two of the greatest powers of Europe, cannot fail to be of much interest to the public, while all who knew him, and especially all who, like myself, had the good fortune to be honoured with his friendship and his confidence, will see in these pages the reflected image of a personality at once stately and genial, robust and refined, and equipped not only with the learning which befits a scholar, but also with all the graces and accomplishments which add such a charm to learning and to power, wheresoever they are found, when they are conjoined with them. Brought up, as he was, in that atmosphere which now appears so fascinating to us all,—the atmosphere which surrounded the old school of American gentlemen at the period immediately succeeding the Revolution,—and under the care of a father, himself one of the most illustrious of statesmen and lawyers which our country has produced, the friend and confidant of James Madison and one of the pillars of his administration, your distinguished father gave early promise of the great reputation which he subsequently achieved among his countrymen.

From his youth up he was acquainted with the cares and responsibilities of public office, and in every position to which he was elevated by his countrymen, he not only displayed great abilities, but also the most conscientious regard for both public and private rights, and that zeal and assiduity in the discharge of public duties which earned the approval of his fellow-citizens and the commendation of all familiar with public affairs. The diaries which you propose to publish were, as you know, read by me long ago, and I found them full of instruction and amusement. Mr. Dallas's pure and honourable life and his agreeable and courtly manners made him always a favourite at the courts to which he was accredited, and often, no doubt, put him in possession of secrets of state which would not have been intrusted to a less popular minister. Hence the diaries are full of interesting facts, while the occasional gossip of courtly circles adds much that is interesting as well as amusing to the reader. These records of the daily experiences and observation at foreign courts of one so quick of apprehension, so versatile, and so competent to impart to them an attractive form in their relation, are records which we could ill afford to lose, and you will deserve, and I doubt not will receive, the thanks, as well as the praise, of all who read this volume, for having given it to the public.

I remain, my dear Miss Dallas,
                Yours very faithfully,
                        M. RUSSELL THAYER.

PHILADELPHIA, September 23, 1891.

AT THE COURT OF THE CZAR.
(NICHOLAS I.)
1837—1839.

DIARY

OF

GEORGE MIFFLIN DALLAS.

1837. *July* 29.—The Independence made Dagerost Point on the evening of Thursday, the 27th instant, and with a brisk breeze on the quarter turned into the Gulf of Finland at about eight o'clock; continuing our course almost before the wind, we reached the last light, the Tolbeacon light, at about ten o'clock last night, and the pilot deemed it most prudent to lay to until dawn, at two o'clock this morning, when we made sail again and anchored in the harbour of Cronstadt at about five. While coming up the gulf, on this side of Horgland, we passed a Russian squadron, principally composed of three-deckers and line-of-battle ships, one dozen in number, with the Admiral of which our Commodore exchanged a salute of seventeen guns. We saluted, after anchoring, with twenty-one guns.

The day has been rendered memorable by a dramatic visit from the Emperor Nicholas, accompanied by the chief officers now here, among them Count Nesselrode, Prince Mensikoff, and the Governor of Cronstadt. The Emperor is fond of these abrupt and covered visitations, and plays the game with dexterity and ease. Our vice-consul at Cronstadt, Leonartzen, happened to be accompanying the Commodore in his gig on a visit to the

Governor of Cronstadt, at about eleven o'clock, when the barge belonging to the Imperial steamboat passed them, and he immediately recognized the Czar acting as its coxswain, and distinguishable from the officers who surrounded him by a close white cloth cap. The gig was immediately turned back in the just belief that the Emperor would come on board the Independence. He first, however, stopped at the Danish frigate lying near us, and remained undetected for half an hour. He then came to us, still acting as a mere aid or subordinate to Prince Mensikoff, and coming last up our gangway. As he obviously desired to pass without recognition, his retinue paid no attention to him, and it was a matter of obvious courtesy with us to forbear breaking in upon his fancied incognito. He separated himself from the rest, peered actively throughout the ship, spoke inquiringly to a number of the seamen, and accidentally coming across my infant daughter, took her in his arms, expressed great delight at her beauty, and repeatedly kissed her.

His fine figure and penetrating eye had been remarked, however, by almost every one, and no one was deceived as to his reality. When going, he touched his cap to Prince Mensikoff, inquired whether he was ready to leave, and, being answered affirmatively, ran up the gangway, descended, and again took the helm, while the ceremony of departure was going through by the others. Our Commodore now broke through the disguise and saluted him with forty-one guns, which induced him at once to resume the Emperor, to hoist signals to the Russian frigate ordering a return of the salute, to run up at the mast-head of his steamboat the American ensign, and finally, to display his Imperial standard. This last act was instantly followed by tremendous salutes from all the numerous men-of-war in the harbour and from the various forts of Cronstadt. The effect was fine beyond description, and our ship seemed to be for a time the centre round which was acting one of the most beautiful and exciting scenes imaginable.

During this remarkable visit I became personally known to Count Nesselrode.

1837. *July* 31.—The Governor of Cronstadt having placed his steamer at my disposal for the purpose, I, this morning, sent all my baggage on board of her, and embarked with my family, accompanied by a number of the officers of the Independence, for St. Petersburg. Commodore Nicholson stayed on board his ship, the Independence, and gave me a salute of fifteen guns. Thus closed my connection with this noble frigate and her gallant crew. It seemed like severing the last cord which bound me to my home, and, with all my family, I own I was deeply affected. The steamer was slow of motion; the navigation over flats and bars, although but sixteen miles, required a pilot; the sun was intensely hot, and we reached the English quay, on the right bank of the Neva, at about half-past four o'clock.

1837. *August* 1.—Much time was consumed in order to prepare for our presentation to the Emperor and Empress on Sunday next, and in examining the house of Monsieur Bobrinski, near the admiralty, which is recommended by our consul, Mr. A. P. Gibson.

1837. *August* 5.—I entered upon the possession of a house I have rented from Count Bobrinski, at the sum of nine thousand roubles, or eighteen hundred dollars, per annum. It is fully furnished, and promises to be alike neat, gentlemanly, clean, and comfortable. The operation of moving in has been laborious and fatiguing; but

I am overjoyed at again finding myself under a roof of my own, with all my children around me, and, as it were, once more at home.

1837. *August* 6.—Mrs. Dallas, my two daughters, and I in one carriage, and Mr. Chew, my secretary of legation, in another, with an extra carriage for baggage, left St. Petersburg to-day at about ten o'clock, and reached Peterhoff Palace by twelve. We were shown into a suite of apartments, and had served up a comfortable *déjeûner a la fourchette*. After putting on our court costume, we were informed that Imperial carriages would conduct us to the palace for presentation at about half-past three o'clock. Accordingly they came. I now rode with Mrs. Dallas in one carriage, and left my daughters to be escorted in the other by Mr. Chew. We were ushered into a splendid antechamber up-stairs, the walls of which were wainscoted with beautiful paintings, at least four hundred different heads, all of great delicacy and nearly the same size.

The master of ceremonies led the ladies into a corner of the apartment overlooking the grand water-works, and I entered into easy conversation with Baron Nicolai. We were almost the first present. The room, however, rapidly filled with glittering officers, military and civil, and with ladies, whose glowing, soft, and fair complexions it was impossible not to admire.

After some time passed in listless expectation and chat, I was conducted into a distant chamber and presented to Nicholas I. I had hardly entered the door before he came rapidly towards me, his hands both extended, and, with an air of great frankness and ease, shook me by the hands with the utmost apparent cordiality. His first words were: "Mr. Dallas, you are welcome to Russia.

I have to thank you for the very handsome and hospitable manner in which my disguised visit to your ship was received. I have never seen a nobler vessel. I found you knew me after I had gone; but did any one recognize me while on board? You were here twenty-four years ago, but you could hardly know me, changed as I am since then. I took your ship on the moment of her arrival, in her ordinary sea-trim: I did not want to see her dressed up. She is an admirable ship. I am going to send some of my naval officers to the United States to learn naval architecture and science; and I must request you to let them have such letters as will facilitate their progress. Can you persuade Commodore Nicholson to delay his departure until after Friday next, when the eighty-gun ship at the new admiralty is to be launched? I should be much pleased to have him present and to hear his remarks."

To all and each of these inquiries I, of course, made replies. He asked me also what the disturbances in Canada were tending to, and observed that when a government became oppressive, and forgot the tender care to which a colony was entitled, she justified resistance and separation.

I told him that I put little faith in the alleged spirit of independence in Canada; that dissatisfaction had long prevailed there; but the people were not, I believe, energetic or united enough for a decisive course of action. We then spoke about Russia, and I said that I had been much struck with the great improvements made during his reign in the department of his marine, especially at Cronstadt; and in the magnificent structures of St. Petersburg. "Why," said he, "I am perfectly satisfied with this people, and will do all I can for them."

At the close of the conversation he again shook me by the hand, and I bowed and left him. I had, during a pause, put my letter of credence in his possession, which he laid upon a table without opening; and, in reply to my assurance that the United States were disposed to strengthen and confirm the harmonious relations subsisting between the two governments, he said that he felt delight at the conviction of that truth, and would not be behind my government in manifestations of cordial friendship. I was immediately afterwards conducted to the Empress, who remarked, among other things, that our government was in the practice of changing its representatives here very frequently, and she wanted to know whether the same course was pursued as to other countries, and whether it arose from any settled principle of policy. I told her that it was indiscriminately done, was partly ascribable to the changes to which all popular governments were more or less subject, and in many cases was imputable to accidental causes. "Well," said she, " I hope you will prove an exception to this practice, that you will be happy in Russia, and remain long."

We had been formally invited to dine with the Imperial family as soon as we reached the palace, and as soon as the form of being presented had closed, and the Emperor, Empress, the Grand Duchess of Würtemberg, and the grand duchesses, daughters of the Emperor, had mingled in the crowd of the ante-room for about fifteen minutes, the doors of the banqueting-room were thrown open, a numerous band of music struck up, and the company proceeded, with apparently very little formality, to dinner.

One of the masters of ceremonies led me forward and placed me at table immediately in front of the Empress, while Mrs. Dallas and my daughters were placed next to the Imperial family, alongside of the younger grand duchess. I was repeatedly addressed, on various topics, by the Empress, who spoke distinct, if not handsome, English. Among her other remarks was her desire to know whether our novelist Cooper had lately written another book, for he was her great favourite, especially in such works as the " Pioneer," the " Spy," and the " Last of the Mohicans." She had, however, not read all, nor, in my opinion, his best productions, and I recommended the " Red Rover" and the " Water-Witch." She had not heard before of his last work on England, and seemed surprised that he should write about a country where he had been so little.

I had cause to be officially and personally highly gratified, and hastened to return to St. Petersburg. We galloped home by nine o'clock, driven by a coachman who was very drunk, but of whose condition we were not aware till safely housed.

I left in the hands of one of the officers in waiting the sum of two hundred roubles, the customary present on similar occasions.

1837. *August* 13.—The frigate Independence sailed from Cronstadt at about noon to-day.

1837. *August* 20.—Attended divine worship in the chapel of the British factory on the English quay. The two front pews have been civilly devoted to myself and family. The clergyman, whose sermon was certainly good, is named Law, and is of the stock of Lord Ellenborough and of Thomas Law, of Washington.

1837. *August* 26.—The Spanish consul here, Don Raymond de Chacon, paid me a visit, to inquire about his brother in Philadelphia. In the course of conversation, he told me there was very little official business for him to attend to here; that, although Spanish produce to the amount of fifty millions was annually brought into Russia from the West Indies or the Peninsula, sugar, coffee, wines, etc., it came in British or American vessels. During all last year but three Spanish vessels came to Russia, to the port of Riga. I asked him news from the seat of civil war, and this led to other general remarks. He says Mendizabel is a very able man, but no ability can compel the Spaniards to pay the levies made upon them for the public service, which cannot get on without money; that the attempt of Don Carlos must fail ultimately, even if he succeed in reaching Madrid; that he is fortunate in having excellent officers in command of his forces, and that his soldiers fight with an enthusiasm and devotion scarcely conceivable; that he is openly countenanced by Russia, who, if she does not, as she in fact cannot, actually lend him money, secretly and efficiently encourages and guarantees others in doing so; and that the pretensions of the people of Catalonia, the principal supporters of Carlos, are so obnoxious to all the rest of Spain, and so utterly inconsistent with the integrity of the Spanish monarchy, that nothing more is necessary than a little additional success on their part in order to make every other Spaniard a soldier for the Queen.

1837. *August* 28.—The Countess de Ficquelmont, wife of the Austrian Ambassador, paid Mrs. Dallas a visit. She is very far the finest-looking woman I have yet seen, her personal appearance being an agreeable combination of Mrs. Maria Watmough and Mrs. Wadsworth.

Our consul brought me cards of invitation to the subscription ball given on Wednesday next at the Palace of the Mineral Waters. It is usually attended, I am told, by the diplomatic corps, and furnishes a fair opportunity for the ladies to see the fashionable world of St. Petersburg.

The Count and Countess Schimmelpenninck (Minister from Holland) called late this evening. He is anything but handsome, but speaks English slightly and French fluently. He is an unaffected, plain man of business, never before here, and confessedly as much like a fish out of water in diplomatic life as I am. He has eight children, the eldest sixteen years of age. He tells me he has rented a house in the Great Moscoy, belonging to Baron Talse, for fifteen thousand roubles. He says that his family have long been concerned in our Holland Land Company, and he manifested some pleasure when I told him that I did not believe the commercial distress of our country would affect the Genesee lands or their farmers.

1837. *September* 8.—Mr. Rodofinikine called this morning; among other matters he referred to the wretched condition of the Russian peasantry, and said that they were in the habit of burying their money, whether silver or gold, and of pretending to be utterly destitute; that four or five hundred rubles was a very large sum for them to own, and that until a recent ukase of the present Emperor they were not competent to hold any portion of the soil, but that now there were about a million of them who owned small tracts of land, which they farmed. He expressed an opinion that too much labour was already bestowed upon agriculture, and that more was produced than could be consumed, and no markets were to be found for the surplus. Great quantities of sheep were raised in the southern provinces, and Count Nesselrode had, in the neighbourhood of Wosnesensk, a flock of about seventeen thousand merinos.

We repeated some of our diplomatic visits to-day, only finding the Countess Ficquelmont (Austrian embassy) at home. I mentioned to her that the United States were about to form diplomatic relations with Austria, and that we should all be proud to see her some day or other in America. She blushed for an instant, and then said that when fourteen years of age (I should suppose her now to be about thirty-five) she had been on the eve of marrying an American by the name of Dulaney, but that her mother had interfered and prevented it; she would otherwise have gone to my country and have there spent her life; and she seemed to recur to its beauties and fertility as to pictures which a young and ardent correspondent had indelibly engraven on her memory.

1837. *September* 10.—The imports of tobacco into St. Petersburg have been the subject of my study to-day. I am satisfied that we supply Russia with this weed to an extent of nearly half a million dollars annually, and that the trade has increased, is still increasing, and might, by modification of the Russian tariff, be very largely increased.

1837. *September* 11.—The ceremony at the monastery of St. Alexander Nafsky attracted us to-day. It is that saint's day, and usually a very imposing procession, after much solemn church performance, accompanies the image of the Virgin Mary from the monastery to the Church of St. Kazan. The Emperor and his court, however, are absent, and things were this morning comparatively flat. The crowd of gorgeously-dressed officers was considerable; the priestly services were protracted, and the throng of spectators in the perspective was long and dense. The badness of the weather no doubt interfered disadvantageously. The church in the monastery is remarkably fine: its lofty dome, finely-arched ceilings, rich altar, countless paintings of uncommon excellence, and the sumptuous silver tomb of the saint, were all sources of much gratification. Nor could we avoid being struck with the music of the chanting, characterized, as it was, by some of the deepest and most powerful voices I ever heard. There must be something in the worship of the Greek Church more impressive than a stranger who cannot understand its language, and, therefore, cannot follow its forms, is apt to imagine. It was singular to see the apparent earnestness and reverence with which, as the consecration closed, the gaudily-dressed officers of state and army and navy, some of whom we knew, hastened to kiss the cross, held mildly forward by the officiating priest, and the external coverings of the saint's monument.

The Saxon chargé, Baron de Seebach, spent tea-time with us. He gave me an animated account of my landlord, Count Bobrinski, who is about twenty-eight years of age and married. His fortune is immense; he takes the lead in munificent subscriptions and contributions to all enterprises of importance, and is distinguished for eccentricity. He derives his principal enjoyment from the excitement of danger,—navigating his boat when the wind is heaviest, and seeking sport in bear-hunting. On one occasion he was fortunate enough to have a fight with a large bear he had wounded, and whose tracks he needlessly followed; he was regularly hugged, torn with claws, and would have been killed, had he not used a knife, handed him by his servant, with great dexterity and presence of mind.

1837. *October* 9.—I visited to-day the Mining Company, an institution devoted to the improvement and study of mineralogy, metallurgy, and kindred branches of natural sciences. It is located in a splendid building on the west bank of the Neva, and forms a conspicuous object as the city is approached from Cronstadt. The collection of minerals and fossils is extensive and most beautifully arranged. Nothing can exceed their neatness. I saw here the largest lump of naked gold, weighing twenty-four pounds; the huge rock of malachite, weighing three thousand four hundred and fifty-six pounds; and a number of beautiful models of celebrated mines, factories, and projected bridges, etc. At present there are two hundred and fifty students in the college, though they can accommodate four hundred. The director, whose name I procured from one of the officers, in order to be able to write to him about the box of minerals confided to my care by Dr. Waggener, of Easton, is General Weixenbreyer.

1837. *October* 10.—I have had to-day a protracted and agreeable call from Count de R——, the Danish chargé d'affaires. Our conversation assumed a cast of peculiar interest to me, in relation to public men, and to the difficulties of acquiring information on the internal condition and administration of affairs in Russia. He expressed a very high opinion of the abilities of Lord Durham, who told him, shortly before he left here, that he intended spending this winter in the south of Europe; to abstain during his return to England from entering into busy politics; and to come again to St. Petersburg in the summer of next year. He presumes that the death of the King, William IV., altered his position and plans in some degree. He describes him as naturally a proud, haughty, and resolute man; well versed in the practice of business; eager to be the chief wherever he is, and bent upon being premier sooner or later. Europe, he thinks, will applaud his moderation in reference to the case of the Vixen, when it is known that, having had it in his power to produce a general war, and being impelled to it by his own ministry and by the inclination of his own sovereign, he nevertheless boldly and effectually pursued a course to maintain peace. He assumed, indeed, an attitude in all his public conduct, of unexampled independence, as well in reference to his own as to this government. He was in the habit, whenever any Russian officer thwarted his views, of going directly to the Emperor, and of enforcing his complaints even so far as, on several occasions, to obtain the dismissal of those of whose conduct he complained. I told him that I thought, after all, his lordship would find his way into the British cabinet, principally on account of his known radical principles, and the expediency of conciliating the radical party. He said that he was in reality a higher-toned politician than Sir Robert Peel, and that his recent abjuration of radicalism was nothing more than a return to natural sentiment from the disguises of policy.

The present Emperor proposes to emancipate the serfs on the Imperial domain, and to confide their government to Kitisoff. The example will ultimately work its way; but its progress must necessarily be very slow, as it will be resisted by the great nobles.

1837. *October* 12.—I accompanied my family to-day in visiting two places well deserving the curiosity of strangers,—the Tauride Palace and the Preobrajensky Church annexed to the Smolnoy Monastery.

The palace is probably but little inhabited now. Its furniture in general seemed old and neglected, and the temperature throughout was disagreeably cold. With the exception of two or three, the rooms are small. The objects of attraction are: First, the banqueting-hall, a spacious colonnade, opening on one side into an extensive conservatory, with a profusion of plants, smooth gravel walks, and fixtures for splendid illuminations; there are beautiful specimens of antique sculpture stationed between the Corinthian pillars and some noble marble vases; the pillars are surrounded by artificial garlands, twining to the dome, and sustaining innumerable lights; the bas-reliefs were crowded and exceedingly fine; second, the collection of paintings distributed through all the apartments, and in one of them arranged in panels so as to cover entirely two sides, is celebrated; the architectural pieces and the city views struck me as the most vivid and true I had ever seen. The enormous picture of Orpheus before Pluto surrounded by the Fates and Judges, with Cerberus charmed into silence in one corner, and the shade of Eurydice impelled forward in the background, seemed to my eye of the French school. There were excellent specimens of other schools; third, the collection of ancient marbles, busts, figures, and groups is admirable; a good copy of the Laocoon adorned the head of the banqueting-hall. Several figures of laughing children were exceedingly delightful, and, fourth, the gorgeous temple of malachite columns, mosaic slab, Siberian porphyry steps, and rich gold ornaments, which occupies the centre of the circular hall of entrance. This is temporarily placed there, and kept covered by an immense round screen that is hoisted by pulleys; it is intended by

Dimidoff as a present to the church now building in St. Isaac Place, in the rear of the statue of Peter the Great.

The Preobrajensky (commonly called Smolnoy) Church struck us all as by far the most beautiful one we have yet seen. The purity of its milk-white polished columns, the exquisite delicacy and grandeur of its dome, the gorgeousness of its altar-piece, fenced in by railings of *cut glass* and loaded with golden ornaments of the nicest workmanship; the splendid paintings in its panelling, the light yet massive folding-doors of carved gold, and the grand delineation of the Ascension upon which the eyes rest as these doors open; the superb canopy of the Emperor when he worships there, and the chaste yet rich slab and its frame erected in memory of the Empress Maria, recently dead; and, finally, the tasteful form given to the many stoves with which the building is warmed,—all conspired to make our admiration more decided and eloquent than usual. I can imagine nothing finer as a spectacle than what must be the appearance of this church on occasions of solemn ceremony, and when fully lighted up.

The river Neva rose to-day, under the influence of a strong wind from the southeast, three feet higher than I have yet noticed it to be.

1837. *October* 15.—Mr. Van Buren's first Presidential message, made to the special Congress convened on the 4th of September last, was in *Galignani's Messenger* that reached me this morning. Thus forty days elapsed before I received this most interesting document.

At so great a distance from the theatre of action, I cannot pretend to speculate, with any confidence, upon the state of politics at Washington. There are, however, two or three conclusions deduced from recent news which I think are reasonable and just. Two hundred and nineteen out of the two hundred and forty members of the House of Representatives were present on the first day: allowing for some imperfect delegations and some sicknesses, the number that attended indicates an active state of the public mind, and a hope, on the part of the opposition, of being able to effect something. Polk had one hundred and sixteen votes for the speaker's chair, and Bell one hundred and three: if, as is probable, neither voted for himself nor for his competitor, then the number present was two hundred and twenty-one. The result indicates a sound condition of our party, generally speaking: so decided a rally for so decided a partisan as Polk is not to be mistaken; and I feel assured that the administration is secure of a steady support. But the majority of thirteen cannot be expected to remain uniform and inflexible as to all measures, and I apprehend secession or independent voting will take place as readily and promptly on the questions respecting the currency and the establishment of government offices of deposit and disbursement as on any imaginable question. No doubt, the election of the speaker extinguishes all idea of a national bank, and so far Mr. Van Buren will be victoriously borne out; but his project of relief—of severing altogether the connection between the national fiscal concerns and the State banks, and of creating officers as means for that end—may be embarrassed, if not rejected. The message is an able paper. In its tone and dignity it is auspicious of a new era; in its extreme length it belongs to the old class. Its decision is admirable, and bespeaks, especially as the production of a most sagacious politician, the strongest possible confidence in the dispositions and will of the people. The President is obviously sure of his ground, and throws his views to his fellow-citizens with all the boldness and the fulness which attest a conviction that they will be acceptable and echoed back. If I mistake not, the time has come for the most important operation of finance ever yet executed in America: I mean the unmeshing the public revenues, and keeping them always, and at a moment's warning, at the control of the people to whom they belong. The whole science of finance will become simplified; all the doubts heretofore mixed up with its movements will be removed; and the commonest farmer will be able to appreciate, with positive certainty, the condition and capabilities of the public treasury. What has the government got in its vaults? will be the only necessary inquiry in order to determine all questions of expenditures.

I have some speculative doubts about this great measure of isolating the public treasury which might probably yield to the suggestions of clearer heads than mine. I can very well perceive all the safety and convenience resulting from the plan, and I feel no sort of apprehension about the pitiful augmentation of patronage or expense. But as a politician whose creed reposes mainly upon the separate State governments and the people, I entertain some jealousy of a proposition which contemplates endowing, not the national executive, but the Federal government, with a treasure absolutely independent of all popular sympathy or local embarrassment. Is it not the beau ideal of American republicanism that the government, participating promptly and keenly in the weal or woe of the people, is therefore perpetually alive to their prosperity? Ought not the government, particularly as to its life-blood, money, to be always embarked in the same boat, sharing in the same hazards, with the mass who are governed? If its treasure be safe on shore, are not its dependence upon, and its attachment to, the crew diminished? Will not the influence of the people upon their government be lessened, if not totally destroyed, when that government has accumulated a vast hoard of wealth, not to be affected or endangered by anything they may suffer or want? Suppose the surplus revenue at this moment to amount to five hundred million,—and ten years of prosperous hoarding would make it equal to that,—and see how practically independent, both of the people and the States, the general government becomes. There would exist a central and consolidated power with a vengeance; a power that would have as little need to attend to the happiness of the people as had Napoleon, with his four hundred millions of francs in the cellars of the Thuilleries, when he meditated the invasion of Russia. It was certainly the doctrine of Chief-Justice Marshall that the general government should always be capable of an absolute, independent exercise of all its constitutional functions; and in the abstract the theory is sound; but, as a Democrat, I doubt whether we should be very vigorous in carrying it into practice. I do not mean that I would be in favor of preserving the connection subsisting between the national treasury and the State bank: the evils springing out of that are positive and overwhelming; but I do mean to say that I doubt whether I would consent to such an arrangement for the keeping and disbursement of the public moneys as would make their safety and availability totally independent of the condition, wants, wishes, distresses, and opinions of the people.

1837. *November* 1.—The acting consul of the United

States, Mr. Van Sassen, called on me yesterday. In course of conversation he stated that he was obliged to meet the Commercial Court at twelve o'clock, of which he was one of the judges, and I obtained from him the following description of this tribunal:

The three mercantile guilds embrace about eight thousand persons. These are all entitled to participate in the annual election of the members of this bench, although, in fact, not more than two thousand take a part. The court consists of one president (now and generally a person learned in the principles and forms of Russian laws), one vice-president (of the same qualifications), and eight merchants. The merchants receive no compensation, and are obliged to serve for three years. The court divides itself, for expedition and facility, into two sections,—one of four merchants, over which the president presides; the other, of the same number, with the vice-president. Their jurisdiction extends to all controversies in the slightest degree connected with and arising out of any transaction of trade, and their decisions are final, if the amount in dispute does not exceed ten thousand roubles. An appeal lies to the senate. Their sessions are secret, each section meeting twice a week and on different days; and the parties litigant may, if they like, employ lawyers, a class of persons here in no repute. The judges have each an equal voice in deciding every cause, and the decision is made by ballot. This tribunal was established by the present Emperor about five years ago; and, as it is a court of record, it has had great effect in systematizing and settling commercial principles and rule. Its expenses are defrayed partly by the Imperial treasury and partly by the city of St. Petersburg.

There can certainly be no lack of materials for correspondence here, for everything and everybody and every usage and every fashion are novel and striking. We are out every day, one squadron of four or five in the carriage, and another on foot, and we uniformly return, after two or three hours' exercise, with exclamations as to the strangeness, the grandeur, the folly, or the beauty of what we have encountered. On one day, an Imperial band of music, several hundred strong, is met in the Nevski Prospective, and our carriage moves slowly for a mile in the midst of the finest airs most finely executed. On another day, the postilion cracks his whip, and we are galloped to a parade-ground and witness the evolutions of two thousand cavalry, the men richly equipped in white cassimere, with helmets fit for Achilles, and mounted on jet-black horses. Again, what carriage is that we are meeting? It is drawn by six grays, with postilions and outriders all in crimson-and-gold liveries, and is that of the Princess Galitzen, who is more than a hundred years of age, and is the revered maid of honor of the present Empress, as she was of the great Catherine II. Again, we will wait till the approaching cavalcade passes by. The moulding of the magical bullets in "Der Freischütz" was not accompanied by a more horrible and grotesque set of figures. They advance in pairs, enveloped in long and loose robes of black, wearing hats with crowns fitted tight and round to the head, and brims at least a foot broad, each man carrying a blazing torch in the clear sunshine. There may be a hundred of them, and in the centre of the line there is borne upon the shoulders of six or eight a bright, gaudy, tinselled, scarlet coffin!

It is not necessary that I should pause to find subjects for description. The commonest and most constantly recurring appearances are singular to our eye and taste.

The streets afford at every step something for comment. Here, for instance, comes a mere labourer. His covering is a sheepskin cloak, the wool inwards, lapping over in front, and kept together by a coarse and often colored girdle. It is dirty externally beyond conception, smeared black with grease, and smells most offensively. He wears a hat of no shape, with the band drawn tight half-way in the crown. His feet are hid in a sort of matting, composed of strips about an inch wide and plaited in the form of a moccason. His beard hangs a foot from his chin. His moustache is thick and conceals both lips, and his hair, coarse and matted, is cut close and round, just along the rim of his hat. His neck is entirely bare, and his skin is everywhere pallid, hard, and dusty. This is an exact delineation of the mass of the serfs or peasants whom you meet by thousands at work along the wharves, or on the public buildings, or at the highways. They are literally " the hewers of wood and drawers of water," and when in the former occupation have a huge, broad, short-handled hatchet stuck in their girdles; when in the latter, they move in pairs, carrying an enormous conical bucket, hanging from a bar of wood, which rests on a shoulder of each. The droschky driver covers his sheepskin with a blue woollen coat, has a black velvet collar and a scarlet belt. The domestic servants indulge in every variety of fanciful clothing. The shopkeeper is more staid in externals, but still prefers the girdled coat, and is inseparable from beard and moustache. The merchants, who are slowly rising in the social scale under the auspices of the existing autocrat, are assimilating to the merchants everywhere. Distinct from all these, distinct and domineering, are the military and nobles,—the military, worthy of personal association only after their ranks have been winnowed; the nobles, spoiled by slavery, are fierce and despotic, but hospitable and patriotic.

1837. *November* 14.—The French Ambassador, Barante, paid us a long visit. He is obviously preparing for a permanent departure. His conversation, always intellectual, was peculiarly agreeable this morning. In speaking of the comparative characteristics of this country and England, France, and America, he was particularly emphatic in pronouncing society in Russia to be listless, sombre, and indifferent or unexcitable. In Paris, people had no time to note the weather or for sickness. Here time hung heavily upon the health and spirits of all but the natives, and they were heavier than time itself. He gave me a brief notice of the Greek minister, Prince Soutzo, who, he said, was in reality unknown to the soil of his own country, having sprung from a family of Wallachia of great distinction, hospodars under Turkish government, and having spent nearly all his life in Paris. He had, however, exhibited great patriotism, made vast sacrifices to principle, and stood deservedly high in the affections of Greece.

I asked him whether he was going home to aid in settling the policy of France as to Constantina. He said it required no consultation or settlement:—it was impossible, without wasteful expenditure, to colonize Africa:—the Arabs could no more be persuaded to turn farmers than our Indians could, and no possible benefit could result from their colonizing their conquest.

He was much surprised to hear from me that Texas was sufficiently extensive to furnish six or seven new and distinct States ultimately to our Union, and presumed that all the Eastern and old States would oppose an annexation which must be followed by the loss of political power in the end. He had adopted an idea from Galignani, and was astonished at my opinion that Texas would, notwithstanding one or two difficulties, be soon admitted as a member of the confederacy.

1837. *November* 18.—Strangers, on coming to St. Petersburg, are apt to be early impressed with the belief that they are vigilantly supervised, even in their domestic recesses and conversations, by the police. Your principal household servants are represented to be secret agents of this body, who will affect ignorance of your language and great personal fidelity, and yet be knowing and dexterous enough to understand and communicate everything to their employers. To me it is matter of no importance whatever. I have nothing to conceal, and entertain no feelings in relation to this government or its masters which would betray me into idle talk. Nevertheless, we all experienced last evening a short fright, arising out of this idea, which may make us for the future more prudent. Mrs. Dallas had occupied the morning in writing to her mother, and had freely expressed some sentiments in her letter relating to the Imperial family and to Russian society generally; just enough, without any harshness, to make the notion of its being seen unpleasant. Called suddenly from her writing, she hastily put her manuscript, with other papers, into the drawer of the table, and was unable to recur to it again until late in the evening. It was not to be found! Every drawer or recess was carefully searched; every sheet of paper was separately examined; behind the sofas, under the cushions, on all the tables, in all the rooms, to no purpose. And yet certainly, most certainly, she recollected having put it in one of the table-drawers, and with some pages of ruled paper, which were there untouched. I began to be worried. I asked to have the contents repeated to me, and did not quite relish the possibility of their being inspected. We have an English nurse, just now in a state of discontent. Could she have seized it for mischievous purposes? We have a new, dark-eyed, silent, and sagacious porter. He had obviously, while we were at dinner, been in the parlor, and had changed the candles on the very table. Could *he* have pocketed the missing sheet? The police-office and its instruments now became bugbears. I had a notion of apprising the whole household of what we found was abstracted, to demand its restoration in the course of ten minutes, or to dismiss every servant at one fell swoop? Mrs. Dallas began her perplexities, and looked upon the probability of its having been stolen with great alarm. After working ourselves gradually, by reflecting upon the possible consequences and by repeatedly searching in all places fruitlessly, into fever heat, when on the point of giving up all hope, I suggested the expediency of taking out entirely all the table-drawers and of looking into their cavities, as the paper might have got shoved behind the drawers, or might adhere to the surface of the table which it came in contact with. Sure enough, there it was, according to the last suggestion, sticking to the under surface of the table, and remaining, therefore, wholly invisible when the drawer itself was opened or taken out. Though at once relieved from our solicitudes, we deduced from the incident a lesson of prudence as to what we committed to paper which will not readily be forgotten; while at the same time it struck me that similar occurrences might often awaken an exaggerated and false estimate of police interference.

1837. *November* 20.—While riding yesterday, at about 3 P.M., we noticed that the bridge which crosses the Neva near the Winter Palace had been floated loose along the opposite shore; and this we conceived to be proof that the ice was coming down from Lake Ladoga, and that the police of the city were making the necessary preparations. This morning the river is filled with large masses of ice, extending nearly from shore to shore, the bridge from St. Isaac's Square to Vasiliosteff has been removed, and the boats alone now afford means of communication.

1837. *November* 22.—Lamartine, in his "Voyage en Orient," describes a semi-official attendant or body-servant among the Arabs very much resembling the *chasseur* in this country. The *carvas* were originally designated by the Sultan to wait on Ambassadors and distinguished travellers; they subsequently were attached to consulates. I am not aware that the chasseur here derives his peculiar functions from the government; he is, however universally and uniformly recognized, and is exclusively associated with diplomatic representation.

1837. *November* 23.—We go to-night to our first Russian entertainment since the dinner at Peterhoff,—the *soirée* of Count and Countess Levachoff. We are invited to come at ten o'clock,—and I presume we will reach there by eleven.

1837. *November* 24.—We remained at Count Levachoff's till between three and four this morning. He is an aide-de-camp of the Emperor, a cavalry general, a nobleman of great wealth, and his personal manners recommend him strongly, at least to a stranger like myself. His palace (for it cannot be otherwise called) is exceedingly splendid, and enjoys the reputation of being one of the most beautiful in this city of palaces. The Countess has the look and deportment of an accomplished and unaffected American lady, and often reminded me of Mrs. Robert Morris, subsequently Mrs. Bloodgood. Both of them speak the English language fluently. I counted eleven rooms, of various sizes and furniture, opened for the entertainment, all brilliant with light, paintings, and decoration. The two largest rooms were appropriated to dancing and card-playing. The order of arrivals and departures at the front door was protected by hussars in couples, and a shoal of most gorgeously-liveried servants superintended every detail within-doors. The Count, in full military costume, met us at the drawing-room door, took Mrs. Dallas from my arm, and led her to the Countess and then to a seat. I was cordially saluted by several whom I had visited but not seen, and among them by my old acquaintance Poletica, who is remarkably unchanged in appearance. Many of the diplomatic corps were there, —the Austrian, Würtembérger, Neapolitan, Englishman, Dane, Sardinian, Saxon, Swede. The company was, however, not large, perhaps not exceeding one hundred and fifty. The Grand Duke Michel was present. I remarked as very striking in figure and expression, Count Orloff. We supped at about two in the morning. Count and Countess Woronzow invited us to their *soirée* of Thursday next.

Count Nesselrode, though he still abstains from his bureau, sent me an invitation, this morning, to dinner on Tuesday next; and we have all received the tickets for the "Assemblées de la Noblesse" which are commencing.

1837. *November* 25.—I went to-night to the "Assemblée de Noblesse." The rooms, nearly opposite the Church of St. Kazan, are sufficiently elegant and commodious; the ball-room is, perhaps, very fine. Of the company that convened, however, I formed an unpleasant impression; they were secondary in every aspect,—a sort of shabby genteel. One of the directors, himself a nobleman, stated that *nobody* was present, and he hoped that I would bring my family to the next, when the Imperial family were expected to attend. I left the palace in the course of an hour, Sunday having hardly begun.

1837. *November* 30.—The *soirée* of Countess Woronzow Daschkaw was resorted to this evening. We went at half-past ten and remained till four in the morning. I met here, and was introduced to him by Count Nesselrode, Count Orloff, whose fine military figure and manner seem to justify the high favour he is known to enjoy with the Emperor. Most of the diplomatic corps were present, among them the Marquis and Marchioness Villafranca.

1837. *December* 3.—The weather has remained open and mild: a slight fall of snow during last night gives a general appearance of winter, and for the first time the little sledges are in numbers substituted for the droschkies, but unless the wind shifts to the north we can have but little frost yet.

My presentation to the Grand Duchess Helen, wife of the Grand Duke Michel, took place at the palace at two o'clock. On entering the door, I was saluted by a company of dismounted dragoons, and ushered up-stairs through rows of attendants into a magnificent hall of reception, supported in its vaulted and richly-painted ceiling by noble columns of white mock marble. Here I remained in conversation with two officers of the household, and admiring the walls and other ornaments of the apartments. I was particularly struck with the glowing and immense paintings executed on the milk-white and glossy walls, and with the uncommonly beautiful mosaic floor. After waiting there about twenty minutes, I was marshalled through a suite of rooms until I reached one of special elegance, in which the Grand Duchess advanced to meet me with much animation and grace. We stood in conversation for fifteen or twenty minutes. Her dress was in nothing striking, except a single enormous pearl of great purity which hung directly in the centre of her forehead below the parting of her hair. We spoke about my family; about her travels during the summer; about the rapid improvements making in Russia under the auspices of the present Emperor; about the annexation of Texas to our Union, and about the possibility of Canada following in the same course. In all she manifested much intelligence and vivacity.

1837. *December* 4.—My set of silver salts and cruets were purchased this morning for one thousand and thirty roubles; and I think I thus adequately furnish my dining-table, having already procured English glass, French porcelain, Russian lights, and English cutlery. My aim has been to unite elegance and taste with as much simplicity as the subject-matter would admit. As to vying, even remotely, with the gorgeous extravagance exhibited by the principal members of the circle in which as a national representative I necessarily must move in this capital, the attempt would be equally out of character, in bad taste, and utterly futile.

I went, accompanied by my daughter, to a *soirée* at the Countess Laval's. It is one of the handsomest and most richly-furnished houses in St. Petersburg. Nothing more strongly shows the magic of wealth. The Count is said to have come here originally as a French hairdresser, and certainly looks the origin at this moment admirably; he is short, mean, and insignificant in appearance. The Countess is the personation of an indented toad-stool,—fat, coarse, short, and ugly. They are, however, both very kind persons and seem deservedly favourites. He is one of the four "Maîtres de la Cour." His establishment presents many points worthy of admiration. It is on the largest scale of private dwellings in a city where all such dwellings are palaces; its various apartments are adorned with the utmost profusion and with great judgment; its largest saloon, an oblong square of about thirty-five by twenty-five feet, with vaulted ceiling, and walls covered with deep crimson satin drapery, is hung with choice paintings of the best Italian and French masters; adjoining this is an apartment of about the same dimensions, whose floor is ancient mosaic from the Island of Capreæ, and whose sides are crowded with specimens of antique sculpture, vases, and curiosities. I noticed especially here a most exquisite antique Gorgon's head, another of Augustus Cæsar, and several that I could not identify,—the money expended in this single room must have been incalculable; beyond this, and after passing a narrow passage, I reached a most beautiful boudoir, modelled with the most elaborate exactness, in all its colours, shape, size, and arrangements, after an excavated chamber of Pompeii. This seemed the pet piece of the Count and Countess, both of whom were eloquent in pointing out its peculiar beauties. There was one display at this entertainment which I have not seen at others, except at the two public balls of the Mineral Springs and "L'Assemblée de la Noblesse:" in the first of the range of saloons as you entered, one side of the room was occupied by an immense table covered with all sorts of delicacies, ices, jellies, fruit, cakes, sugar-plums of all colors and fantasies, coffee, chocolate, wines, liqueurs, and which was the fountain whence the attendants afterwards distributed on waiters to the company, or to which the gentlemen resorted whenever inclined for refreshment. Cards, particularly, if not exclusively, whist, were playing in four or five saloons; and Countess Laval, with entire composure, executed a most skilful game of chess with Count Litta in the very midst of her guests in the most thronged saloon. The party was what is here called a rout,—without dancing,—beginning at eleven o'clock and closing in less than two hours, and it was composed chiefly of married ladies from thirty to seventy years of age. I should not suppose there were four girls, as we would call them, present. The dresses were exceedingly handsome, but some of the matrons shocked my American notions not a little by a most profuse display of the bust. Conversation does not seem to be as much a pursuit as it should be; generally speaking, gentlemen arranged themselves in a dark mass on one side of the saloon, respectfully and vacantly gazing at the ladies, who were closely packed on divans, ottomans, or sofas, on the other side or in the centre. The diplomatic body are an exception to this remark, and seem disposed to make themselves agreeable to their fair associates.

1837. *December* 10.—The Neva was thronged with ice, which continued, however, in motion until about three o'clock, when it fastened.

I was yesterday and to-day particularly struck with the brilliancy of the moon, which, at about half-past three P.M., shone with that clear golden light we would expect in the United States to see at about nine at night.

1837. *December* 12.—Yesterday, crowds were constantly

walking over the Neva upon a wooden platform laid on the ice, starting near the admiralty.

1837. *December* 17.—Corréa, the Portuguese chargé, spent the evening with us, and made himself exceedingly agreeable. He mentioned that General Dearborn had been very much liked at Lisbon; that he dressed with all the simplicity of a Quaker, with his long, white hair hanging about his neck, and was an object of great popular deference whenever he appeared in the streets; that the King was extremely partial to him, always shook him by the hand as a personal friend, and on one occasion begged him to accept as a present a gold snuff-box, surrounded with brilliants, estimated at a value of forty thousand pounds, but the General declined, as officially prohibited, and, being pressed to take something as an old friend, said he would accept the old gloves of his majesty, which were accordingly given to him. The snuff-box was afterwards reduced in its costliness and presented to another member of the diplomatic corps.

1837. *December* 18.—This being St. Nicholas Day, and therefore the "*Name's Day*" of the Emperor, it is the subject of universal celebration. Count Nesselrode has a multitudinous dinner at the "Hôtel du Ministère d'Affaires Étrangères," to which I am obliged to go, "Selon les Usages," in grand uniform; and in the evening, as I was formally apprised by the secretary of the court, Mr. Maikailoff, some days ago, the Ball of the Nobility will be attended by the Grand Duchess Helen, and all are expected to dress their loftiest. The city, generally, also undergoes illumination at night, and the Neva consecration.

1837. *December* 19.—At Count Nesselrode's dinner, yesterday, all the diplomatic corps attended except Luchenfeldt, of Bavaria. On such occasions established etiquette requires that Ambassadors and Ministers should take their seats at table according to the precedence arising from the dates of their respective arrivals at this Court, Ambassadors, of course, as higher in grade, being before Ministers. I took my place next to Mr. Milbanke below, and, as I presumed, above Count Schimmelpenninck. In the course of the evening, after we had risen from the table, the Dutchman informed me that he disputed the right of Mr. Milbanke to the precedence he assumed; that he had spoken to Count Nesselrode upon the subject, and to Mr. Brunoff, and that both these gentlemen were inclined to agree with him in the views he expressed, and promised to communicate to him their formal decision on the point. The result would, of course, affect me by advancing me one step in the line should the conclusion be against the British representative. The grounds of his proceeding are simply these. Lord Durham was Ambassador, and, on quitting Russia, he left Milbanke chargé d'affaires, an appointment since confirmed by the British government. As chargé left by an Ambassador, Milbanke ranks as a Minister Plenipotentiary, and took that rank before either I or Count Schimmelpenninck reached here; but he is not an Envoy Extraordinary, and that is *our* most important and distinctive grade, and the Count considers it essentially higher than the mere Minister Plenipotentiary, and therefore entitling us to precedence. It would seem, also, that Milbanke is even Minister Plenipotentiary more by a sort of diplomatic *brevet* than by actual commission in *the line;* and his personal deportment appears to have kindled a disposition to pull him a little back from the forward position he too boldly takes.

At the "Assemblée de la Noblesse" all attended, in honour of the day, "*en grand costume.*" The effect was striking, but somewhat fantastical.

1837. *December* 22.—The Imperial standard waves this morning over the Winter Palace,—the silent proclamation that the autocrat is again here. He probably arrived during the night.

1837. *December* 25.—Received two New York newspapers, confirming the entire defeat of the Democracy in that State at the elections in November. Is this State, then, relapsing into its former character for instability and veering? I remember well that, until the success of General Jackson, the politicians of Pennsylvania scarcely ever thought it worth while to count New York one way or the other: they had an invincible impression that she pursued no principle, and was just as liable, in following the lead of her clannish families, to be against as for the Democracy. She has relapsed—or collapsed— with a vengeance, and I do not see how her "favourite son" can reconcile it to himself to proceed without her. He must either abandon his post or his policy; and of the two, I mistake his character if he would not prefer the former. Were I in his position, I should be irresistibly impelled to this course: *first,* because it would indicate a just submission to the voice of popular suffrage; *second*, because it would be an *éclatante* manifestation of his disinterestedness as to office, and perfect sincerity as to the opinions heretofore expressed; *third*, because, as a stroke of policy, effective by its novelty, it would probably make its actor the rallying-point of a new struggle in which I could not doubt ultimate and glorious triumph. It would be analogous, though in a much wider sphere and upon less purely party grounds, to the withdrawal

of Mr. Rives from the Senate and his victorious return.
But my impulses are not exactly such as govern statesmen generally : so nothing of this sort need be looked
for; and I must confess that I fear being mortified by
finding the administration quarrelling among themselves,
weakened by changes, and timidly yielding to the panic :
I hope not, but I dread. Suppose, however, that this
extraordinary and unexpected result in New York be
but the forerunner of an overthrow to the Republican
party in the Union, and the reinstallation of Federalism.
The calamity will be great as regards the character and
progress of our institutions : we shall retrograde rapidly ;
but the evil cannot, in the nature of things, last long, and
the people may be taught a wholesome lesson of moderation for the future. As to my particular self,—although, I
dare say, this result would be thought specially mortifying
to my feelings and disastrous to my fortunes,—I should
really not care for an opportunity to prove that sunshine
is not essential to my well-being in any point of view.

1837. *December* 26.—I dined to-day with Prince Butera, the Neapolitan Minister. He married a Russian
widow of immense wealth, owning productive gold mines
in Siberia. His residence on the English Quay is one
of the most splendid establishments I have visited.
There were present the Austrian and French Ambassadors, the Prussian, English, and Dutch Ministers, Count
Woronzow, Count Matuzewitch, the French secretary
of legation, the Marquis de Villafranca, and a French
attaché. The table was brilliant and the dinner exquisite, especially the dish of Neapolitan macaroni and
the glass of Imperial Tokay. During the repast much
conversation of a lively character took place respecting
Madame Taglioni, whose dancing, last evening, enchanted

the Emperor and Empress. On this topic the Austrian was poetically eloquent, and described the feet of the actress as actually speaking. He insisted, also, that her extraordinary length of arms greatly contributed to her grace and activity, being admirable substitutes for the balance-pole employed by tight-rope dancers. The Marquis de Villafranca and I, after being introduced, had a long and interesting confab. He is not an unapt-looking representative of the Spanish Pretender, Don Carlos. Of about forty years of age, short figure, round limbs, jet-black hair and eyes, bushy moustache, and swarthy complexion, he looks the young but grave grandee. He has heretofore represented his country at Naples and Vienna in different capacities, and has now been absent from it for eight years. He is modest and unassuming, and seemed quite conscious of the peculiarity of his position here. He had been well acquainted in early life with the Yrujos; recognized the old Marquis from the manner in which I described his figure and gait, and said that his son, a man of decided talents, after being employed abroad, was likely to be distinguished as a statesman at home. He did not exactly know how either the Yrujos or the Tacons sided in the present civil war in Spain.

We prepared, this evening, the "Travels of Miss Martineau in America" as a present for the Grand Duchess Helen, as she particularly requested a loan of the book from Mrs. Dallas, at her presentation. I don't half like giving circulation to the production, as if specially sanctioned by me, although it certainly has much merit, and is, with some exceptions, reasonably fair; but it cannot be avoided without making the matter of much more importance and formality than is at all necessary.

I crossed and recrossed the Neva upon the ice to-day, and was amused by seeing the preparations making by a body of men for an extensive skating plain. Trees were planted in the ice on the line of demarcation; some benches were already stationed; the snow was shovelled and wheeled off, and through a hole cut water was procured and thrown in buckets over the appointed space, thus securing a smooth and clean surface. On returning home, while walking carelessly with Philip along the English Quay, a single-horsed small sledge approached at a rapid pace, with apparently one of the numberless military officers in it, whom we see in all directions, enveloped in a light-blue cloth cloak, and with cocked hat and feather, and speeding exactly in the same unattended and simple manner. I did not notice, much less recognize, the person in the sledge until after he had made the usual gesture with his hand (putting it to the side of his hat by his forehead and there retaining it), and had nodded repeatedly at me, with smiles, as if endeavouring to make me know him. I had just time to whip my hat off and turn towards him most respectfully: it was the Emperor of all the Russias! He flew rapidly by, and I observed that all who were in his track seemed aware almost by instinct of his approach, and doffed their hats and caps instantly. Here was the monarch of myriads —the despotic arbiter of life and death and liberty and law—actually and visibly enjoying the *sleigh-ride* in a style as entirely unassuming and fearless and natural as would be chosen by any one of his subjects or slaves. The constitutional king, Louis Philippe, could not venture on this without the music of whistling bullets being awakened, and even a king or queen of England would run some risk of violence or rudeness. Yet such is the every-day practice of Nicholas the First. He is probably bold in the consciousness that he strives to do his duty, or the excessive degradation of his slaves prevents the least hazard of a generous aspiration and struggle for liberty.

1837. *December* 27.—Dr. Lefevre's second lecture on chemistry was delivered this evening, and I accompanied three of my children to it. At its close we went to Mr. Law's, the English clergyman, nephew of Lord Ellenborough and our Thomas Law, and remained till midnight. My daughters danced to the music of the piano, while I took my seat at a card-table and won from his reverence at whist ten roubles! How strangely different are the religious prejudices of different countries! Mr. Law dresses in black, and in that alone, when out of the pulpit, differs from any of the crowd of gentlemen who may meet in the ball-room, the theatre, or at the green baize!

1837. *December* 28.—Dined at Prince Hohenlohe's; meeting the French Ambassador, his secretary, D'André, and his attaché, Marquis Darchiac, the Neapolitan Minister, General Narischkin, Count Borch, General D'Apotchinine, Mr. Rianhardt, and another gentleman whom I did not know. The service of china was singular: a first set, for substantial eating, of English, light-blue figured Liverpool ware; the second set, for jellies, etc., a splendid series of paintings on porcelain, representing the principal views of Paris; and a third set, very delicately finished, seemingly of Dresden, each plate containing a coloured picture of a village or chateau. This last struck me as peculiar, and I examined the back of the plate and found that all the scenery and houses represented, numerous and various as they were, were described as " Appartenant au Prince de Hohenlohe." As I sat near him, I expressed my admiration of a delineation of an ancient chateau, beneath which were written in gilt letters "*Orient*," and he immediately said it was the place of his birth.

As to the cookery, it was signalized by one dish, "*Un pouding a la Richelieu;*" the *carte* lay near me, and I discerned its title. The rest was good, but not wonderful, not as recherche as Buteras. I have yet to accompany the ladies to Count Woronzow's *soirée*.

1837. *December* 29.—We were gratified last night by finding the Emperor among the guests at Count Woronzow's. He had told the Count when at Moscow that he would attend his parties, provided that they began at nine o'clock; the Count feared that was an impossibility: his Majesty went, however, at the hour he had indicated, and was alone until nearly eleven! Fashion is more potent than autocracy. When I entered the room where he was, I perceived him to be in conversation with Count Schimmelpenninck, and forbore to advance: he caught my eye, left the Count, and coming towards me we shook hands, when he observed that he had met me two days ago; that I obviously did not recognize him, but that he never saw any person for five minutes whom he afterwards forgot.

The Winter Palace is just reported in flames!

1837. *December* 30.—The great Winter Palace is now a quadrangular stack of blackened and gloomy walls; still, however, at twelve o'clock to-night blazing in every direction with almost unabated fury. As a spectacle, it is more grand and imposing than any exhibition I ever beheld. The Emperor has ordered all dangerous efforts to arrest or extinguish the flames to be abandoned, and the noble pile, with its gorgeous and rich contents, is left, surrounded by an army in full costume, to consume itself away. The whole scene is the celebration of the obsequies of some mighty monarch. As yet, the origin of this calamity is merely matter of conjecture and rumour; but one story has an air of verisimilitude, and is generally credited. Some persons are said to have been engaged in the apothecary's apartment in making chemical experiments, and having accidentally ignited a quantity of fluid, the blaze extended itself and gradually became irrepressible and inextinguishable. The Emperor was, at the time, in the theatre, witnessing the graces of Taglioni, and hurrying home, he arrived at the palace at the moment when the fire burst forth from several points. This immense conflagration has in no manner disturbed the general tranquillity of the city. No bells have rung, no outcry has been made, no noisy engines have rattled along the streets, and no crowds have been collected. The process of supervising it being allotted to the military and police, the operation has been conducted with the silence, system, and despatch by which those two departments are characterized.

I did not retire to bed this morning until some of the household servants were bustling about preparing for the day. Circumstances, over which we sat brooding, had excited vague alarms in all the family. In despotic governments, fears of conspiracy and change are always more or less afloat. The agents of the police keep these fears alive, as necessary to their own importance. Some of the French newspapers had contained a statement that a plot against the Emperor was being actively followed up. He went to Sarsko-Selo for some days, on his return hither, instead of taking up his quarters at once, as he was wont to do, at the Winter Palace. Then he moved about without attendance or parade, as witness the manner in which he appeared at Count Woronzow's *soirée;* and we recollected, furthermore, many harsh things said of his extreme and passionate violence in the reviews at Wosnesensk, and especially towards a general officer of noble rank, whose badges of honour he rudely tore from his breast with his own hand in the presence of the troops. All these ideas, when aggravated by the light of the burning palace, would probably have given way to farther reflection, had not, as if to invigorate and confirm them, a notice been sent me from the Imperial Guard that two other large fires had broken out in distant quarters of the city; that a doubt existed whether they were not the explosion of some general plan, and that I was desired to be vigilant in the care of my own household. I was on the point of revisiting the palace a second time, when I met the soldier at the door who gave this notice to my servant verbally. We were now countenanced, in some degree, in indulging our imaginations, and we very soon worked our way into the midst of a revolution and the conflagration of the city. I sent for the secretary of legation to take charge of the archives of the mission, stationed my servants at the points most suited for effective lookouts, and tranquillized the family as well as I could. The extraordinary silence that prevailed was, however, the great restorer of intellectual composure, and I got all to bed by two o'clock, except Mr. Chew and myself, who remained up and on the *qui vive.*

EXTRACT FROM A LETTER.

"DEAR MARIA,—The vast Winter Palace of the Czar has been blazing, unchecked and irrepressible, for sixteen hours, and will soon be a mass of black ruins!

The richest, strongest, proudest regal residence of Europe is no more!

"The fire broke out at about ten o'clock last evening. Jumping into a sleigh, I reached the palace square in ten minutes, but a military cordon was already formed, and I could advance no farther. Silence the most profound reigned everywhere,—no outcry, no bells, no roaring of engines, no alarm of any sort; nothing below to be seen but the flitting of police-officers on sledges, and the hurrying of coaches and four to the palace doors, while, above, the bright volumes of flame, augmenting and spreading every moment, illuminated the whole heavens and shed a most disastrous glare over the city. Even curiosity seemed to be lulled, for, except at one or two street corners, not a group to be seen!

"As soon as we had breakfasted this morning, the carriage was ordered, and we have *en masse* just returned from gazing upon the still blazing windows of a pile within whose walls we had promised ourselves a succession of delights during the present winter. Its interesting and precious wing or detachment, the Hermitage, built by Catherine II., and the repository of the finest existing collection of paintings, jewels, and curiosities, has been preserved by early cutting away the flying gallery which united it to the palace. The fire seems to relish its dainty food, and will not quit the repast before the expiration of at least forty-eight hours. It would be idle to speculate thus early on the origin of this disaster. Some pretend that it burst out of the four corners of the building at the same moment, and others that it was kindled just beneath the Emperor's chamber. The fact is, that his Majesty was at the theatre witnessing the graces of Taglioni; and that if a design existed against his person, it was developed at a most unseasonably early hour of the night. Nor can I see any motive for plotting against the present sovereign; such a plot must necessarily be in the hands of the nobility and army, for as to the mass here, they are as yet nothing. What good can the Boyars or the soldiers promise themselves from removing an able, indefatigable, and ambitious chief, in order to hasten the reign of his son, who is young, amiable, and rather dull? They cannot hope by any possible change to get a sovereign so admirably fitted for Russia in her actual condition, and so capable of pushing onward her European ascendency. It is worthy to be told of him that when he reached his burning palace, after quitting the theatre, and heard that two or three men had been killed in the effort to extinguish the flames, he instantly exclaimed, 'No more of that; human life is infinitely more valuable than human treasure. Let the building consume, and only prevent its extending.' The worth of this can only be fairly appreciated by those who know the incalculable amount of wealth that has been expended upon and amassed within the palace. The value of the contents is estimated at forty millions of pounds sterling!

"The disquietude created in my household by this event was considerable, and has scarcely yet subsided. Circumstances gave it intensity; and as we talked them over, our conviction became rooted that the town was destined to conflagration, and that we were in the midst of a revolution. There had been much said of the Emperor's violence at the reviews of Wosnesensk. Then a French newspaper had intimated that a conspiracy was tracing. Then on his return to this capital, instead of taking up his quarters at the Winter Palace, as he was in the habit of doing, he remained at Sarsko-Selo, an Imperial château about fifteen miles in the country; then, again, he had made his appearance at a ball of Count Woronzow's the night before, at which we were all present, in a manner wholly unexpected, unattended, and remarkable; then, and still worse, two immense fires burst out in distant quarters of the city, instantaneous with that of the palace; and worse than all, while we pondered over these signs, I received a notice from the Municipal Guard that the conflagrations were extending; that they did not know whether they were accidental or otherwise, and I was requested to be vigilant in securing my own house. I forthwith summoned out of his warm bed, half a mile off, the secretary, to stand by the archives and public documents. I stationed the chasseur at one point, the porter at another in front, and the maître d'hotel I specially charged with supervision of the stable. I remained on the *qui vive* until five in the morning, and though the glow of the sky seemed to increase and expand every moment, and I reveried myself into the conviction that Maelzel would soon have a counterpart of his masterpiece of Moscow, I thought I could neither expedite nor retard the catastrophe by throwing myself on the bed and forgetting all anxieties in sleep."

1837. *December* 31.—Dined to-day at the Princess Bellozieskoy's, meeting Count and Countess Schimmelpenninck, Baron Palmstjerna, General and Countess Zukazanet, etc. Our hostess ranks very high in the first circle of Russian society. Her family, wealth, and hospitality give this distinction, besides being, what is esteemed extremely, a maid of honour, a *portraiss*, to the Empress. Everything in her establishment bespeaks vast resources, and an inveterate attachment to old fashions, old furniture, and massive ornaments. Three separate groups of sporting Cupids of solid silver constituted the central decoration of her dining-table, looking ponderous, rich, and beautiful, also.

1838. *January* 1.—The incidents of the conflagration are rapidly developing and engage at present every attention. The number of lives lost is differently stated: some carry it up to more than two hundred, others to eighty, and a general in actual service on the fatal night explicitly assured me that but one man had been killed. A body of grenadiers are represented to have perished by the sinking of the floor at the moment they were endeavouring to remove and save the throne; and the Emperor is said not to have abandoned the hope of extinguishing the flames until he saw the staff of his standard which surmounted the palace blazing, when he lost colour for a moment, and exclaimed that it appeared to be the will of God, and he would no longer hazard the lives of his officers and subjects in the attempt. He disappeared for a short time from among his attendants, who were alarmed at his absence: he had gone into his private cabinet to collect and secure his private papers, with a large bundle of which in his hands he then came out.

There were nearly four thousand permanent occupants of this immense palace, many of whom were entirely dependent upon this sanctuary for their means of livelihood. Numbers of young ladies attached to the court as maids of honour, or in other capacities, have been suddenly deprived of all their jewels and little property and made destitute; several of them, in their extreme terror, fled from the scene, and were not found again for forty-eight hours, having taken refuge among their friends. Much of the most valuable furniture has been rescued: the Hermitage, which remains untouched; the interesting collection of portraits which covered the walls of the Historical Hall of the Generals was saved by a regiment of soldiers who devoted themselves to that particular object; the crown jewels were early sent away; the Empress, after her return from the theatre, went in person and preserved her own jewelry. The splendid malachite vase, esteemed one of the most precious articles, resisted by its weight and fastenings the exertions of sixty men, and was lost. No attempt was made to sever the gorgeous jasper columns which adorned the saloons of the Empress from the walls, and they are reduced to power. The estimated loss is fifty millions of roubles, or ten millions of dollars. Orders have already issued for the rebuilding, and the Emperor has said that he will reoccupy the palace next September,—utterly and absolutely impossible!

I am informed this evening that a new ministerial department is about to be created, with General Kisileiff at its head. It is exclusively designed for the government of the private domain and properties of the crown, which have latterly been injuriously neglected: a matter of no inconsiderable importance, when it is recollected that the Emperor actually owns about eighteen millions of peasants, or one-third of the population of Russia. This enormous acquisition has been caused by the loans he made after the French war to the nobles, which being unpaid were followed by seizures, etc.

1838. *January* 5.—In the last received number of *Galignani's Messenger*, I perceive among the reported discussions in the British House of Commons that Spring Rice, the Chancellor of the Exchequer, defending the extravagance of the civil list against the attacks of Mr. Hume, has grossly assailed Mr. Stevenson and his legation generally, whom he describes as a "*gaudy array of American officers*" at the levees of the Queen. The insult is so gross and so utterly unwarranted, upon gentlemen who really sacrifice their own tastes and feelings in order in some degree to adapt themselves to the rules and costumes of the court, that I think our government should notice it. Certainly, were I in London, the Chancellor of the Exchequer should explain and retract as publicly as he has insulted, or Lord Palmerston should know that I would thereafter not again appear at court except in plain attire.

1838. *January* 6.—The President's message reached here to-day. As Congress met on the 4th of December, and the message could not well have left New York before the 6th, it has crossed the Atlantic and Baltic in less than thirty-one days. While on a visit to Count Nesselrode this evening, I was told by Count Laval, Count Schimmelpenninck, and Count Nesselrode that they had received this document. Neither of them, however, had read it. The American Minister, who ought to have got it first and would have devoured it greedily, was obliged to accept a loan of it from one of these gentlemen.

Agreeably to the note I yesterday received from the master of ceremonies, Count Woronzow, I was, at two o'clock to-day, in due form, presented to his Imperial Highness the Grand Duke Michel, eldest brother of the Emperor. Mr. Chew accompanied me. Several other diplomatic functionaries underwent the same process while I was there. The Grand Duke is seen to advantage when more closely approached, and impressed me, certainly, more favorably as to his manners, intelligence, and personal appearance than he had done before. There was nothing in our conversation worthy of a memorandum.

1838. *January* 12.—One of the most beautiful objects which I have noticed as developed by the frost, in the scenery of St. Petersburg, is the monument of Peter the Great, in St. Isaac's Square, as it now appears. For two or three days there has been much fog in the atmosphere, which, collecting uniformly and gently upon the icy-cold surface, presents the most splendid creation of frost-work imaginable. The granite rock, the rearing horse, and the noble rider, are all equally and purely white. The shades are finely displayed, and, at a little distance, viewed with a dark cloud behind, the whole realizes perfectly a colossal specimen of the newly-invented medallions. A similar effect is produced upon the Alexandrine Column, which looks like an unbroken shaft of exquisite alabaster. The rows of trees, too, in front of the Admiralty and of the Gostenadvor are picturesque beyond description.

1838. *January* 13.—This is the New-Year's Day of Russia, and an active interchange of personal civilities takes place. Cards are sent to all one's acquaintances.

The Court convened at the Palace of the Hermitage at twelve o'clock, to celebrate, agreeably to my note and invitation, the anniversary of the birth of "*Her Highness Helen.*" The ceremonial is one deemed peculiarly high and important, and the occasion rallies all the Court, all the civil functionaries, and all the military officers, together with all the maids of honour, to the presence of the sovereigns. I made it a point to reach the palace-door punctually at the hour designated, accompanied by the secretary of the legation. It was instantly obvious that the vast basement accommodations of the Winter Palace were no longer to be had. The door, though not obstructed, was flanked by throngs of liveried servants, whose masters had passed in, and the stairway was equally crowded. On my name being announced, an attendant, dressed fancifully as a highlander, presented himself as our guide, opened the mass of human beings in our way, and marshalled us through two lines of richly-apparelled gentlemen and officers, along an extensive corridor hung with the finest paintings, until we reached the saloon appropriated for the meeting of the foreign Ministers. On entering, I found the corps diplomatique assembled, with the exceptions of Prince Butera and Count Schimmelpenninck, who, however, soon appeared. We were all in full costume, and Counts Nesselrode and Woronzow were with us. A folding-door at the extremity of the room, opposite to where we had come in, being suddenly thrown wide, we were gratified by beholding an immense array of ladies of honour, dressed in the rich and gorgeous national costume which has been prescribed by the present Empress. The apartment in which they stood was large and beautiful, and they moved about with ease, and thus exhibited their fine figures and finer ornaments to entire advantage. The trains were mostly of crimson, purple, or light-blue velvet, embroidered in gold or silver, and dragging about two yards upon the floor. The head-dress was a variation of the ordinary Russian nurse's cap, a peculiarity in attire which was very becoming; it was composed of every kind of material, and of all varieties of colour. Diamonds, pearls, emeralds, topaz, etc., jewelry of all descriptions, seemed to have been showered upon each of the ladies. We arranged ourselves in a sort of semicircle, with the Austrian Ambassador at the head, and according to the rank of seniority. Our secretaries stood behind us respectively, and soon the approach of the Emperor and Empress from the interior of the palace and through the splendid saloon before us was felt. The gentlemen of the bedchamber, with coats covered with gold embroidery, white buckskin pantaloons, shoes and buckles, and chapeaux and gloves, first moved by us in a throng of about two hundred, going out at the opposite door, and halting at the entrance. Then came the high officers of ceremony, Litta, Laval, Narischkin, etc., with their appropriate attire and insignia, who ranged themselves on our left, by the side of Nesselrode and Woronzow. These were immediately followed by the Grand Duchess Helen, wife of the Grand Duke Michel, the Grand Duchesses Marie and Olga, and their two younger nieces, daughters of the Grand Duke Michel, who, in a line fronting us, stationed themselves on our right, the Grand Duchess Helen being within easy speaking distance of Count Ficquelmont. Following these Imperial ladies were the Grand Duke Michel and the Grand Duke Heir, who, as they entered, turned a little to the left, and left the way clear for the Emperor and Empress. As their Majesties entered, we all bowed, first to the lady, and then to the monarch, and the former advanced to the Austrian, offered her hand for the usual kiss, and conversed for a few moments. She was victoriously equipped: her train of sky-blue velvet, embroidered with silver flowers to the depth of two feet, was protected and occasionally adjusted by two pages, who followed her in the garb of young lieutenants; her cap, in shape and meaning like that worn by the maids of honour, was decorated by rows of enormous pearls and diamonds,

and appeared to be of cherry-coloured satin; her gown
was of pink satin, richly embroidered in gold; and her
necklace, bracelets, rings, etc., were brilliant in proportion. As soon as she left the Ambassador, the Emperor
advanced to him, shook hands cordially, and talked with
animation. His dress was that of a general, unincumbered by glitter; his coat green, his epaulettes gold, his
pantaloons white buckskin, fitting tight to the skin, and
his boots, long hussars, eclipsing Day and Martin by
their polish. On these occasions, the sovereigns pass
slowly down the line of diplomats, addressing each as
they like in succession. When my turn came, I kissed
the hand of the Empress, and expressed my gratification
at perceiving that her summer travels had improved her
health. She said they had on the whole, but just now
she felt exceedingly unwell; that she had not recovered
the shock of the conflagration, and was utterly unfit to
go through the labours of the day; that, according to
established rule, she would be obliged to receive and
shake hands with about four thousand persons, and, being
then scarcely able to stand from faintness, how was she
to get along? I told her she really looked very differently from what she felt, and expressed my sincere
regret; but that perhaps the delight her presence would
inspire might react upon herself and give her strength
and spirit for the scene. The Emperor shook me by the
hand, and at once asked me why I had not been at
Count Woronzow's party on Thursday; that he had seen
Mrs. Dallas and my daughters there, but looked in vain
for me. I told him that I had gone, unfortunately for
me, too late; that I had been occupied (as in truth I had
been in preparing for all the emergencies that might
arise on my interview with Count Nesselrode) until past

eleven o'clock; but that, had I been aware that I should have met his Majesty, no engagement should have detained me. He said, with a smile, "The plain truth is, you are more fashionable than I am." The Empress spoke to me in English, the Emperor in French. After completing the semicircle, and being then by the door, they both turned round, gave a salutation to the corps generally, and left the room, their attendants all following. And then came, in one splendid and prolonged sweep, with a magnificence of rustle and smile altogether overwhelming, the whole cavalcade of maids of honour, giving to us a rare and surpassing review. When the door closed, we were at liberty to depart, and I hastened to my carriage, eager to reach home and divest myself of my stiff uniform.

In the evening we went *en masse* to a ball given by Mrs. Harder, the married daughter of Baron Steiglitz. The ladies returned home before midnight, resolved not to invade their Sabbath; but at one o'clock in the morning I carried off Mr. Chew to the masquerade at the Great Russian Theatre, and continued there, without amusement except such as is afforded by an idle, motley, musical, and strolling crowd.

1838. *January* 15.—Countess Laval's first ball was to-night, and we repaired to it. Her magnificent dwelling expanded still farther than I ever noticed it before: a new series of splendid rooms was opened in addition to those heretofore described, and ended in a vast dancing-saloon, with superbly arched ceiling, lighted by two immense bronze chandeliers and side candelabras—wax candles in all. No supper; but a large apartment with two tables kept loaded all the evening with refreshments. Card-tables innumerable, and all occupied.

1838. *January* 18.—*La Fête des Rois*, and the consecration of the Neva under a pavilion opposite the Hermitage and through a hole cut in the ice, performed by the Emperor. We started to witness the proceedings at half-past eleven in a crowded carriage, and drove at once upon the frozen river, and within two hundred yards of the pavilion. It was thronged with priests in their sumptuous garments, and with military officers who brought their respective banners to be dipped in the holy flood. All present stood uncovered while mass was being performed. The vast multitude collected for the occasion could not be less than forty thousand in number, and those gathered immediately round the scene of consecration, and in a compact mass upon the ice, I presumed to be about twenty thousand.

1838. *January* 19.—At noon went to the Emperor's private Palace of Annitchkoff, high up the Nevskoi Prospekt, and was in due form presented to his Imperial Highness, Monseigneur the Grand Duke Czarovitz Heir, with whose fine form, soft countenance, and unaffected good manners I was highly prepossessed. His destiny is a striking one, but I should much question his possessing the bold and resolute qualities of the will, as well as the active intellectual ones, without which he must be a sad and uncertain successor to his father. We were introduced by Count Woronzow, who seems to limit his services as grand maître des ceremonies personally to the Emperor, Empress, and heir. Mr. Milbanke preceded me, and I was followed by Count de Rantzau, Baron Seebach, Marquis de Carrega, Count de Sersay, chargé d'affaires, and by Mr. Chew, Counts Chazelle, D'Archaic, Gerard, and D'Appony, as secretaries and attachés. The whole thing was over in less than an hour after quitting my home.

Apprised by De Sersay that our diplomatic set of *ice hills* at the country residence of Count Laval were ready, I drove Phil and my daughters forthwith to visit them. We were all delighted with the amusement. Two parallel and nearly adjoining straight platforms of beautifully clear and smooth ice, formed of distinct but inseparably united blocks of uniform width and depth, run in opposite directions for perhaps two or three squares, and rise gradually at their opposite extremes fifty or sixty feet high into the upper chambers of two fanciful pavilions: the line separating the plains is a mound of soft and clean snow, of sufficient elevation to prevent it being easily surmounted in the progress of the sport, and the outer boundaries are similarly composed. Very small and exquisitely neat and showy sledges are employed, with runners generally of polished steel, and with light and narrow cushions of differently coloured velvet, or worked worsted, or red morocco; each accommodates two persons, and a lady may seat herself in front of a gentleman, with her feet a little lifted and pointed the course she is going: the start from the pavilion is precipitous, and, of course, requires no external impetus; the velocity is extreme during the greater part of the transit; the course is governed by the gentleman, whose hands are covered with thick, stuffed gloves or gauntlets, and who, leaning a little back, by the slightest touch upon the ice guides the vehicle with the nicety and precision which characterize the effect of a rudder upon a skiff; the sledge is arrested gently or abruptly, according to the skill of its manager, at the end of the plain and at the foot of the other pavilion, into which the parties mount by a stairway with their feathery apparatus, and taking a fresh start in the reverse direction shoot back to the foot of the pavilion whence they first issued. The going and return may occupy two or three minutes, and seemed to be accompanied with great exhilaration and delight to the voyagers. The cold was severe, and we had somewhat too much wind; but my children, who immediately and fearlessly engaged in the excitement, were much pleased. There is no real danger, though awkwardness and failure in the descent may cause vexation, as they give rise to loud mirth in the spectators.

1838. *January* 20.—Went to the ice-hills, but the weather was too cold and windy for the amusement.

Dined at the Austrian Ambassador's. Met there the Countess des Champs and her nephew, Baron Palmstjerna, Baron Seebach, Colonel Terchky, who leaves for the Caucasus in two days, Count D'Appony, Kaiserfeldt, and two other officers whose names I do not know. Madame Hitroff took the seat of her absent hostess, whose ill health will not permit her to be at table. Madame Hitroff is the daughter of the illustrious Kutusoff, who resisted and defeated the invasion of Napoleon in 1812-13. She bears a striking resemblance to her father, but is not handsome enough to be recognized as the mother of Countess Ficquelmont.

1838. *January* 23.—Dined at Baron Palmstjerna's, the Swedish Minister's, meeting the Austrian Ambassador, the Würtemberg do., the Dutch do., and a number of Russian gentlemen, among whom I knew only Baron Brunoff, Count Woronzow, Mr. Narischkin, the two brothers Prince Dolgorouky and Prince Dondankoff Korsakoff. In the course of conversation, the Austrian told us an animated anecdote of his crossing the Alps on a particular occasion, just after the road on which he was travelling had been completely overwhelmed by an extensive avalanche; that the peasantry perceived that it would be an almost endless job to remove the snow by hauling in carts, and therefore resolved to tunnel it; and in fact had cut a square avenue directly through a distance of two hundred feet, that his coachman drove straight forward, and that his calèche, being an inch or two higher than the excavation, peeled off with great regularity from the top that quantity of snow, so that he was completely buried in his own vehicle when he emerged from the tunnel. He says modes of directing avalanches, so as to make them in their fall project beyond and pass over the traveller, have been successfully employed of late years.

At half-past seven, I repaired to Count Nesselrode's, with Mrs. Dallas and Julia. It was a grand and select ball to the Imperial family, and the early hour of meeting was designated to suit the health and medical advisers of the Empress. The two sovereigns, with their son the heir, and the Grand Duchess Marie, and the Grand Duke Michel, arrived at about eight, and when the company had, in expectation, collected in the dancing-room. They instantly on entering led off a polonaise, the Emperor with Countess Nesselrode, the Empress with the Austrian Ambassador, and all who could procure walking partners joined the procession, which wound its way through the suite of apartments twice or thrice. I first led Countess Schimmelpenninck and then Countess Laval. The Empress formed a cotillon at the head of the room, and danced repeatedly with much apparent spirit and enjoyment. She participated also in the frolic and waltzing of the mazurka at the end of the evening. The cordial manner in which both the Emperor and Empress addressed me, and the length of time each remained speaking to me, seemed to produce quite a sensation in the crowded and brilliant circle, to whom I was but partially known, and to whom my plain blue coat and white cravat must have appeared singularly unattractive. The Emperor, among other ways of indicating his disposition, raised his voice several keys louder than usual, and said to me, "You are the first gentleman that has ever induced me thus publicly to speak English. I hope you will now undertake to teach me, by frequent conversations, how to speak it well." "With all my heart," was my reply, "though you really speak it so distinctly and correctly already, that I have little or nothing to teach. I will, however, undertake anything, in order to be frequently honoured by your attention." Shortly after this interview, the Grand Duke crossed one of the longest rooms, came directly up to me, and shook hands. He said he had met me the day before yesterday, while he was in a sledge, and I on the English Quay, and that I had not recognized him. "How is it possible for me, an utter stranger, to know you when, without a single attendant, you drive along like any private person, muffled up completely in your cloak and covering your face from the cold? As soon as you lifted your hand, and thus in some degree uncovered your face, I hope your Highness perceived that I knew you instantly." "No doubt, no doubt. The truth is, I prefer moving about without escort. I think we are the only reigning family in Europe who attempt it. It is impossible for me, as a military man, to leave off my uniform, and to divest myself of these tell-tale ornaments (epaulettes and orders), but I should like to avoid the notoriety consequent upon them." The Empress asked me as to the personal appearance of the Queen of England, saying, "I hope she will be great, for she cannot be beautiful. A queen must be tall. A short queen is unfortunate."

All the diplomatic body were present, the Austrian alone in his uniform. Mr. Milbanke treats the Canada affair as a light matter, already ended. I told him he was too sanguine; there was obviously greater concert and enthusiasm among the insurgents than he imagined. "But what can they do?" said he. "They have no army, and, as soon as spring comes, we shall have a force of twenty thousand men there." "That," said I, "will be both very expensive and very formidable." He was obviously not well informed as to the character of the Canadian population, nor as to the measures of his own government to repress the insurrection, and was drawing upon that delightful braggadocio confidence with which Englishmen, in everything and everywhere, anticipate and predict the success of their country.

Our supper, at half-past eleven, was as rich, *recherché*, and gorgeous as possible. Prince Narischkin told me that he had himself purchased at Paris the golden and malachite ornaments of the table, and had given ninety-five thousand roubles for them. He subsequently sold them to the Emperor, who gave them for the use of his Vice-Chancellor.

1838. *January* 31.—We went to the ball of Princess Beloselsky at half-past seven. The Imperial family were all there. The exterior of the house in the first story was illuminated by innumerable lamps. Four hundred and fifty guests were accommodated at the supper-table. The magnificence of the whole scene is indescribable. The stone staircase, branching off at the first landing and leading to the second story, was, in its vastness, ornaments, and style, worthy of the splendour to which it introduced one. After the company had collected in what seemed to be an endless suite of drawing-rooms, another suite, embracing an immense picture-gallery, was thrown open for dancing, and finally, beyond this, another and still more noble series were displayed for supper. The picture-gallery contained many very fine originals, especially of the schools of Correggio and Annibal Carracci, and one, Judith with the Head of Holofernes, by Andrea del Sarto, particularly struck me. Numbers of the subjects were too indelicate, and ought to have been removed on this occasion. Suffering as I did during the whole evening with a pain and fever in my head, I felt no disposition to partake in the gayety around me, and less to converse: my chief occupation was, therefore, in examining the paintings and statuary. In the apartment appropriated to engravings, of which the collection in portraits is extensive and remarkable, I was surprised agreeably by seeing one of Trumbull's of the Battle of Bunker's Hill. While musing silently and in a retired niche, I was agreeably surprised by the Emperor's coming to me, shaking hands, and then leaning against the wall as if disposed to a little chit-chat. I asked him, in allusion to what took place between us at Count Nesselrode's, whether he was ready to take his first lesson in English. He said he hoped to benefit by frequent conversations with me, and repeated emphatically the assurance that I was the only gentleman by whom he had ever been induced to speak the language publicly. I expressed myself highly flattered. He then asked what I thought of the state of things in Canada, and intimated that he had heard of my doubting whether the insurgents had among them a single man competent to lead them. He obviously referred to my interview with the Vice-Chancellor. I asked him whether my opinion had not already been confirmed by the last intelligence? as Papineau, Brown, Mackenzie, and Nelson seemed to be all flying, after having betrayed the cause to which they were attached by mutual jealousies, and by precipitate demonstrations easily put down. Still, I thought the matter was not ended, as the public meetings which took place on the American frontier in my own country indicated a greater confidence in the rebellion than I could explain, while the measures and language of the English governor manifested strong apprehensions of a protracted, if not desperate, struggle. Besides, in London, Lord John Russell seems to have no idea that the affair is over, but, on the contrary, is preparing quite a formidable army for immediate shipment. The Emperor said that it was neither his temper nor his policy to rejoice in the misfortunes of other countries, even though they might be supposed beneficial in their tendencies to the interests of Russia; but, added he, almost in the very words repeating the sentiment he uttered when I presented my letter of credence at Peterhoff, if the mother-country will act oppressively and unjustly towards her colonies, they are right to resist. I told him I thought it would be on the whole the better policy for England to consent to the separation and independence of Canada. "But where then is she to get her timber?" "From the Baltic," I replied. "Yes," he said, "she might, but perhaps not of such good quality, nor as cheap." This drew my mind to his fleet off Cronstadt, and I hazarded the remark that I should like to see those fine-looking ships of his out in the Atlantic. "Why," he replied, "I will probably send some of them there; but really I am charged in all directions with such ambitious projects and such mischievous designs, that I am averse to do anything that, in the slightest degree, might countenance these imputations." "Send a small squadron to visit us," said I, "in the United States. I assure you we shall give them a most cordial welcome." "I should like to do so," he answered, "and think I will send one or two; but my men, who make such good soldiers, make poor sailors." "Give them, or some of them," I observed, "the opportunity of good long voyages and of a bold sea, and they will rapidly improve." The Emperor then invited me to accompany him, as soon as the opening of the navigation in the spring would permit it, on a visit to his Baltic fleet; an invitation which I, of course, accepted. I forgot to record that when he adverted to the accusations commonly made against him, I interrupted him, as apologizing for them in some degree, with the remark, "But, then, you are so powerful, that you naturally inspire jealousy." "Yes," he said, "we are powerful; only, however, for defence, not for attack;" and he seemed anxious that he should express this last idea distinctly, for he quit English, for an instant, to give it in French.

I became this evening personally acquainted with Count Cherchineff, the Minister of the Department of War. He is said to be distinguished by great ability and energy. His figure is tall and stout and well proportioned; his head and face rather small; his hair, eyes, and moustaches peculiarly black; and his complexion somewhat pallid. His department exacts infinite labour. I told him that we had repeatedly interchanged visits and cards without meeting, and that I had ascribed it to his incessant engagements. He said I was right; that such an empire as this, with such a military system, required inconceivable exertion, especially with an Emperor who entered into all the details of business. "For instance," said he, "here I am at midnight, but I must be up at five in the morning, and must meet the Emperor at nine. I have been eleven years in my present post, and can't tell how I live through it all!" I should presume him to be about fifty.

It would seem as if my journal were to be taken up with the descriptions of entertainments and conversations at them. This is not surprising when the season is recollected, and when it is also borne in mind that matters of information are almost inaccessible here except in the manner described.

1838. *February* 3.—The *soirée* and ball of Count Koutchilieff-Besborodko took place to-night. We went there before ten o'clock. He is a widower and the son of Chancellor Besborodko, remarkable for his desire and exertions to collect choice furniture; and truly the house contained rich specimens of his taste in abundance; some of the bronze pieces and many of the paintings are admirable. The suite of rooms is extensive and attracted general curiosity. The stairway, formed of inclined planes, not steps, especially adapted for the safety of children and winding to the upper stories by a series of light square galleries, was novel and beautiful.

I played a game of chess with Countess Laval, and was after a long and interesting fight beaten by a king, knight, and pawn. The Prince of Oldenburg was civil enough to have himself introduced to me without formality. He is a prepossessing young man, lately married to a niece of the Emperor, with a Danish countenance, projecting nose, light flaxen hair, large blue eyes, and delicate complexion; his height is below the ordinary one.

We hurried home early in order to avoid a breach of the Sabbath.

1838. February 7.—We dined with Mr. and Mrs. Hodgson at half-past five, and at eight rose from the table, leaving our entertainment partly unfinished and a numerous company, in order to be early enough at Count Levachoff's, where the Imperial family were to be present. We reached the count's, and were ascending the stairway when the Emperor and Empress and Grand Duchess Marie overtook us. So that we just saved our distance. We got home pretty well tired of our day's exploit at one o'clock in the morning.

I played chess with Count Litta, the crack performer of the highest circles here, and beat him. This at once establishes my reputation; it does more; it affords me a resource at these *soirées* much better than the one of gambling at whist, to which I am so generally persuaded, and to which the lack of something to kill time with strongly tempts me. The extent to which gambling is carried with this sober game of whist is surprising. One gentleman of the diplomatic corps told me that he frequently played for twenty thousand roubles a game, and that last year he lost about eighty-five thousand roubles. Ecarté, too, is constant, and I have noticed many thousands changing owners at this sport in the course of fifteen minutes. At large entertainments twenty or thirty card-tables may be readily counted,—all actively going. I have, however, noticed but one disagreeable scene of conflict, and that ended tranquilly and liberally.

1838. February 9.—A prevalent disease here, among ladies particularly, is the tic-douloureux. It is ascribable to the severity of the climate and to the habit of exposure. Its origin is a cold. One of the most distressing cases now attracting general sympathy is that of the young, beautiful, and universally admired Ambassadress of Austria, Countess de Ficquelmont. She has for some years been subject to it. Her recent attacks, however, are appalling in their severity. The complaint has lodged in her throat and jaws, and she is utterly disabled from swallowing. She has now for eight days been lying on her back, her mouth open, her eyes sunk, and incapable of taking sustenance, of speaking, or of sleep. Latterly, strange to say, but I have it from the indubitable testimony of Mr. Kaizervelt, the secretary of the embassy, she has for three nights in succession avoided the paroxysm by animal magnetism; as she feels the prefatory agitation, she writes a direction for the physician, who immediately attends and magnetizes her short of the point of sleep. She has tried all other remedies in vain, nor is it supposed that this of magnetizing does more than assuage the nerves; cure seems to be hopeless unless she is taken to Italy, the country of her youth and of warmth.

1838. *February* 16.—The splendid ball and supper of Count Woronzow, at which he entertained the Imperial family, opened this evening at half-past seven o'clock. Opposite the door, on the River Neva, and extending the whole width of the house, was an illuminated scaffolding, hung with innumerable lamps. The apartments were numerous and brilliant beyond any former entertainment we have witnessed at this nobleman's; and his guests in greater crowds and more showy equipments. The company of Horse-Guards officers appeared in their fullest costume of scarlet and white, and the uniforms generally were particularly studied in honour of the birthday of one of the Emperor's sisters. The chief supper-room, oval in its form, was arranged with elegance and taste. I should presume that there were plates laid for at least five hundred.

I very soon heard, in the course of the evening, the intelligence, which has reached here through the *Berlin Gazette*, in relation to the attack made by Sir F. Head upon the Canadian insurgents on Navy Island in the Niagara River, his having routed them, and his having pursued an American steamboat, which was said to be engaged in their service, killed her crew within our jurisdiction, set her on fire, and allowed her to drift over the falls. The incident is a stirring one, and is regarded here as involving an outrage upon the sovereignty of the United States, which cannot be overlooked. There is obviously a general dislike of English policy and pretension, and everything is eagerly caught at to fan a quarrel with her. It is impossible, however, without humiliation, to submit to the proceeding of Sir F. Head. The killing of such of our citizens as joined the insurgents on Navy Island is certainly no cause of complaint; the destroying of the steamboat, if she were engaged in the same service, was an act perfectly justifiable, even if she had the impudence to hoist the American flag within the limits of British Canada, and Navy Island is within them; the Governor had a full right to murder, burn, sink, and destroy without incurring any responsibility towards any other nation. The point then merely is—but it is a vast and vital point—that he did not confine himself to the boundaries of Canada, but pursued the insurgents into our limits, and there inflicted the punishment he might well have inflicted on Navy Island. He had no right to follow his criminals—his alleged traitors and rebels—on to our jurisdiction. *He has violated our territory*, and thus inflicted upon the United States as gross an insult and as great a national wrong as it was in his power to inflict. I trust the patriotism of my fellow-citizens has shown itself even without waiting for the action of the national government; but I feel quite sure that, however averse we may be to war, the administration and Congress will be prompt in vindicating the honour and security of the country. Some analogy may be conceived to exist between this conduct of Governor Head and that of General Jackson, when, in 1818, he pursued the Seminole Indians into Florida. The cases are, however, very different, and principally in this feature. Spain had expressly stipulated by treaty to pervent, by force, any Indians within her territory from committing any outrage, invasion, or war upon the adjoining territory of the United States: she distinctly, after remonstrance, admitted her inability to fulfil this stipulation, and that her power was inadequate to control the savages; we were, therefore, driven by the necessities of self-defence to do what Spain had engaged but was unable to do. We crossed the line only after in vain invoking the Spaniard to perform his covenant, and after repeated proofs that as fast as the Seminoles were beaten back into Florida, and our soldiery retired, they would recruit their strength, and return to renew on our soil their butcheries. Nothing of this sort extenuates the proceeding in Niagara River. We have never stipulated to prevent our citizens engaging in any enterprise they please out of our limits. We have never stipulated to surrender traitors or criminals on demand, and if we had, no demand was made for them, and it was clearly not necessary to the self-defence of Governor Head that he should chase a boat within our waters, and then destroy her and her crew.

1838. *February* 17.—Went at half-past ten to a masked ball at the "Assemblée de la Noblesse," and remained without being entertained till near one o'clock in the morning. Nothing can be more stupid. The Emperor and Grand Duke Michel, and it was said some of the Imperial ladies, were present. The ease and fearlessness with which the first moved about showed how little he apprehended hostility towards his person. I *remained* though I did not *go* alone.

1838. *February* 20.—The carnival commenced yesterday. This morning I rode around the Champs de Mars, a large vacant square by the summer gardens, in which have been erected all the temporary buildings usual at this season for the amusement of the people. Heretofore these structures were put up in the square fronting the Admiralty; but it was thought on the present occasion that the sight of the ruins of the Winter Palace would mar the popular pleasures. Neat ice-hills have been prepared, flying-horses, swinging-geese, booths for jugglers, houses for theatres, and the exhibition of wild beasts and tumbling. I went too early and found nothing doing. Adjourned, therefore, to the Imperial Library, situated on the Nevskoi Prospekt, between the Alexandrine Theatre and the Gortenadvor. The locale is fine, and the arrangement internally admirable. Everything seems in capital order, as if not frequently disturbed. We walked slowly through the apartments, and were struck with the quantity of volumes assigned to the department of Russian literature. It probably is more bulky than valuable. All agree, the Russians themselves, that their language is yet in its rude state, and but imperfectly understood. Another room was crowded with Latin works, and is exceedingly precious to the eye of a scholar. We looked through its shelves, and occasionally examined a volume with great interest. Some of the editions are equally rare and ancient; one of Pliny was printed in 1483, only thirty-four years after Gutenberg is supposed to have put the art in full operation at Mentz, and it certainly looks as well executed as the ordinary books of the present day are. We were so much taken up by this collection that we had no time to do more than examine some rare manuscripts, with a great mass of which, of extreme interest, this library has been enriched. I noticed about fifty folios bound in red morocco, which contained autographic correspondence of European sovereigns and ministers during the last eight hundred years. Finding that our curiosity was intent, one of the persons attached to the institution addressed us in French, and politely offered to exhibit some of the rarest morceaux. He put before us a small collection, most carefully secured and protected, of the original letters of Queen Elizabeth, of England; and assuredly I feasted for a while on the character of her writing and the emphasis of her signature; one autograph letter of Richard the Third, the crookback tyrant, several of Charles the First, who was paving his way to the block, and a number of James the First. He then showed us some beautiful illuminated manuscripts, among which that which attracted us most was the prayer-book, in Latin, of Mary Queen of Scots, with her own signature on the first page, and with many couplets of French poetry written by her in the occasional blank spaces; here and there, too, she had made her visitors write their names, and the signatures of Essex and N. Bacon were conspicuous. The tone of her rhymes indicated that they were composed while in prison. The pictures with which the book is embellished are numerous and glowing. In this same department we observed a collection of instruments for writing in glass cases—from the reed to the stile and the pen, and from the dry, broad grass to the papyrus and bark in all their modifications. Two fine full-length portraits of the Emperor Alexander adorn the opposite extremities of the library, importing that he actively and liberally contributed to its advancement. The number of volumes, General Alenine, the director, informed me, was about four hundred thousand. It must be visited again and again and again before it can be justly appreciated.

1838. *February* 21.—In the evening we repaired to the ball of Madame Boutourlin at about nine. The Emperor and the two Grand Dukes, Heritier and Michel, came in the course of the night: the first danced a quadrille with our hostess. After shaking hands, I expressed myself pleased to see that he still danced. He said he was too old, but that an old sentiment of attachment to the lady had got the better of him. "Certainly not too old," said I, "because you are several years younger than myself, and have not got one of the gray hairs by which I am surmounted." "Yes," he replied, "my hairs are gray,—the few I have,—and this (pulling the curls on top) is a perruque." The rooms opened were numerous and furnished beautifully. The pride of the owner lies in his collection of paintings, which he bought in Italy, and some of which are exquisite. I think his Titian, Christ bearing His Cross, over the large sofa of a deep crimson satin saloon, very much the finest I have seen in Russia, and worthy to be a companion of the same subject by Carlo Dolce which I saw at Stratton Park, Sir Thomas Baring's. A marble head of a satyr by Michael Angelo was arranged for great effect, and attracted much notice, but did not equal my expectations of that master: it may be the very head which he copied when but sixteen years of age, and which elicited so much applause as a promise of genius from contemporaries.

On conversing, to-day, in terms of admiration of some of the things I had seen at the Imperial Library, Count Lerchenfeldt informed me that many, if not most, of them had been obtained from the libraries of Polish nobles whose estates had been confiscated. I had noticed a Polish name in many of the volumes.

1838. *February* 22.—Dined at Mr. Sebastian Cramer's. Met Admiral Hamilton, General Ovender, and Mr. Pezanovius, with others. The dinner was execrable. A dancing-party assembled at ten. We left them at half-past ten, and repaired to Princess Butera's. Nothing more beautiful, rich, and tasty than her salon of cut crimson velvet tapestry, with white and gold chairs and settees, splendid mirrors and lustres.

1838. *February* 23.—Thermometer remains the same, and the temperature in the middle of the day agreeable to a rapid walker. At about noon I went on foot with Philip in search of amusement, which, during carnival, seems to be pursed by all Russians, high and low, with untiring assiduity. We first made our way to the Great Theatre, and found it crammed so as to be wholly inaccessible. We then hastened to the French Theatre, or Theatre Michel, and that also was full to overflowing. As a *dernier ressort* we proceeded to the Champs de Mars, intending to look into all the booths and frames devoted to popular gayety. We got into the temporary circus, after paying an enormous price for admission, and, having waited in the cold for half an hour, were content with the first appearance of the wretched troop of riders and hurried out. The ice-hills attracted our attention for a short time, and we travelled through the throng of pedestrians and carriages, but were soon convinced that the chill of the circus made a rapid walk homeward the most agreeable proceeding we could adopt.

1838. *March* 11.—Yesterday, after spending all day in writing, I repaired, conformably to a card of invitation, to the Imperial Institute of St. Catherine, which is of the first distinction as a seminary for the education of the daughters of the nobility, and over which the Empress specially presides as patroness. The triennial examination and display of the quitting class took place. It continues for two or three days in succession. Etiquette required me to go in full costume. We reached the place at a little after seven in the evening, and found the magnificent colonnaded hall filled to overflowing. I managed to squeeze a pathway, however, through the dense crowd to a range of front seats secured for the diplomatic corps. The young ladies, all uniformly clothed in plain white with broad crimson sashes and bows, were in number about one hundred and fifty, went through their exercises of public examination very well, and then sang and danced with much harmony and effect, but no beauty or grace.

1838. *March* 12.—The weather for a week past has been steadily moderating, and is now beautifully fine. The thermometer scarcely indicates at any hour during the day a degree of cold equal to five of Réaumur, and for a fact, it is doubtful whether a general thaw is not proceeding even in the shade. In places exposed to the heat the snow and ice are dissolving.

We went, at seven o'clock, in grand costume, to be

received by their serene Highnesses the Prince and Princess of Oldenburg, who reside in a delightful palace adjoining the Austrian Ambassador's on the Great Quay. There was not the customary stiff state. They are a young couple, married in June last, and apparently happy in each other. His manners are engaging and plain, and hers polished and cordial. His figure is devoid of attraction,—short, and but poorly adjusted,—his hair is light, his eyes round and blue, and his nose aquiline. Her face has much beauty in it,—remarkably fine teeth, good nose, rich flaxen hair, and clear, large blue eyes. When she speaks her countenance is lighted up with smiles and intelligence. We sat down, an unusual circumstance, and conversed for about half an hour.

1838. *March* 14.—Weather still improving.

Much faith prevails here in animal magnetism. Having no belief myself, I was much surprised to hear, this evening, from Mr. Corréa, on whose intelligence and veracity every reliance must be placed, the incident of actual personal observation and experience which has compelled him to credit what he had before totally repudiated. He was in Germany, and in the neighbourhood of one of the towns witnessed an accident to a lady with whom he was well acquainted: she was thrown from her horse, her head severely cut, and she remained insensible. A physician was sent for, who, after anxiously examining, was unable to ascertain the cause of her prolonged insensibility. He proceeded to magnetize her. Corréa, ridiculing, remarked that nothing could be done that way. "Yes," said the physician; "wait a moment, and I will hear what's the matter with her and how best to treat her." In a short time, though still apparently lifeless, the lady spoke, directed attention to particular wounds, and prescribed in Latin (a language unknown to her out of the influence of magnetism) the medicines and applications most suitable for her relief. "I do not," said Mr. Corréa, "ask your belief in this statement. I never could have believed it had I merely heard it from another, but I actually witnessed what I have stated, though I am utterly unable to comprehend it."

1838. *March* 17.—Being specially invited, I dined to-day with ".The English Club," an association formed in 1770, which consists now of more than eight-tenths who are not English, though it embraces all the respectable merchants and traders of that country residing here. They are a wealthy society, and seem bent upon enjoyment. About three hundred persons were at table. It is the anniversary of their foundation. I had hoped to have met Marshal Paskevietch, the Prince of Warsaw, one of the present race of great men of Russia; he had arrived here the day before yesterday, but was not able to attend. I met Sir James Wylie, who has been eminent as a physician, and still continues at the head of medical science in this country. He was chief physician during Paul's and Alexander's reign to the Court and Army. He is a hearty, broad-looking Scotchman of more than sixty-five. The toasts were five: 1. Our Master, the Emperor; 2. The Heir to the Crown, Empress, and all the Imperial Family; 3. The Prosperity of Russia; 4. The English Club; 5. The Queen of England.

1838. *March* 19.—Mrs. Dallas and I at half-past four repaired to Prince Youssoupoff's to dinner. The establishment is on the grandest and costliest scale. The endless range of lofty saloons, the countless paintings upon the walls, the masterly and exquisite statuary, and

the numberless servants gorgeously dressed out in green
and silver, with pages having caps and flowing feathers,
altogether overwhelmed one's faculties of admiration. It
redeemed its reputation of being the largest private residence in St. Petersburg, and far surpassed in splendour
anything I have yet seen. I should suppose there could
not have been less than a thousand paintings of the
various masters, and some of them of immense size.
For two alone, the present Emperor offered two hundred
and fifty thousand roubles, but the sale was declined.
That, however, which riveted my gaze was the noble
piece of sculpture of Canova, Cupid embracing Psyche;
it was placed in the centre of a circular apartment whose
roof was a dome, and whose walls were tapestried in
glowing scarlet; the effect upon the white marble was
beautiful. Our dinner was all that boundless wealth
could make it. The guests were fifty in number: Counts
Orloff and Woronzow, Prince Mensikoff, Princess Beloselsky, Countess Laval, Sherbatoff, Bloudoff, Ministers
of Prussia and Sweden, etc. The dining-hall, of spacious
dimensions, was on one side decorated with family pictures, and on the other with the family plate tastily
arranged in two glass-covered cases, which filled the
whole space, and which, being divided into shelves, ena-
bled one to see every curiously worked piece distinctly,
and to take the whole magnificent service in at one
coup d'œil. The fashion of collecting family plate and
of thus displaying it has recently been borrowed from
England. In a glass mahogany case immediately behind
the seat of our host was preserved the autograph correspondence of Peter the Great. Among other varieties of
the table was a fish which had been brought from a distance of more than two thousand versts. I observed

two waiters carrying a porcelain dish about nine feet long and two wide, and being seated next to my hostess, I inquired what the monster could be; it was more than two yards in length, was of delicate flavour, and tasted to me like salmon; its name I forget. When we left the dining-room, cards were resorted to by some; but Mrs. Dallas and I, after a fresh survey of the paintings and statuary, and having taken coffee and liqueur, came home to prepare to accompany our two girls to the *soirée* of Countess Laval.

At Countess Laval's, I saw for the first time General Paskevietch, Prince of Warsaw, the hero of two wars, Persian and Polish. He was playing whist, and I, therefore, declined interrupting him in order to be introduced. His display of orders and ornaments was brilliant and unusual.

1838. *March* 22.—Having determined on purchasing a carriage and pair of horses, I yesterday traversed various streets, and found my way at last to the common horse-market which is about three miles off. It was crowded with animals of all descriptions and pretensions. I selected a promising pair of bays, and directed them to be brought to my house this morning at ten o'clock. The price asked was a thousand roubles, and I might probably have got them for seven hundred and fifty. As a matter of additional precaution, however, after I had satisfied myself by the opinions of competent judges as to their age, strength, and soundness, I directed them to be harnessed to a carriage for trial. They were put to, but would not budge; they were unbroken and wholly unfit for use! I left the jockey in disgust.

1838. *March* 23.—A fine pair of grays were brought for my inspection this morning, from an extensive stable which I visited yesterday. The young man who had the management of the concern accompanied them. I had them carefully examined, tried first separately in a sledge, and then together in a carriage; we were all much pleased with them, and I bargained for a purchase. I was asked two thousand three hundred and fifty roubles. I offered eighteen hundred, and finally it was agreed that I should have them for nineteen hundred, and that they should be left with me for three days for further trial. They were to be warranted sound. I paid the usual earnest called here hand-money, and ordered my coachman to put the horses up. The whole matter being concluded, I prepared to issue forth for the carriage and other essential adjuncts. When I had reached the street with my *maître d'hôtel*, an old man suddenly stopped us, and as owner, disclaimed the contract made by his agent, professing himself unwilling to sell at the price agreed upon. I walked quietly back into my chancery, while the dispute proceeded in a language I could not understand. In a short time my servant brought me the hand-money, saying that the owner was dissatisfied. I directed him to tell the owner plainly—for I perceived at once the arrangement between the principal and the agent to get more money—that he might take his horses and go the devil! I again heard some loud talk in the hall, and opening the door, ordered my servant to turn the owner, to whom I pointed, instantly out of the house. He immediately perceived that he was understood and foiled, and begged to receive back the hand-money and to execute the bargain. My choler, however, was up, and I felt it to be my turn now to improve the purchase; so I peremptorily refused unless he accepted my original offer of eighteen hundred roubles. He remained in the court-yard some time hesitating, but finally went away slowly with his horses. This morning he returned with them, but I did not see him.

1838. March 25.—Mahlon Dickinson retires from the Navy Department in June next, owing to the increasing infirmities of age, and I am wished at home in order to take his place. Shall I suggest my readiness to obey any summons to that effect? There are many reasons pro and con; but on the whole I am inclined to believe that, being now across the Atlantic, I had better remain tranquil some time longer. If I could persuade myself to believe that my being in the Cabinet could be useful to the country or to my political friends, I would not hesitate upon the sacrifice; but the appointment may perhaps be more advantageously given to an Eastern or a Western man. A Virginian might well be selected. Woodberry is from the East, Butler from New York, Forsyth and Poinsett are both Southerners, and Kendale is Western.

1838. March 31.—We visited the Imperial Manufactory of Mirrors and other Glass, starting at half-past eleven, and not reaching there, unfortunately, till after the workmen had broken off and probably gone to their dinner. The distance is not more than three miles. It will be necessary to repeat our visit, as we were conducted through the extensive range of buildings, and were satisfied that in all respects it merits full examination. We witnessed single processes of making decanters and tumblers, of gilding and painting ornamental pieces, of cooling and grinding smooth, immense plates of looking-glass, and pressing the quicksilver on the back, of cutting bottles, etc. The collection of articles for sale is neatly and attractively arranged, some of them very beautiful. We made a small purchase of two table ornaments of little value, but pretty. I had no servant with me capable of speaking any language but Russian, and was therefore wholly at a loss.

Attended the *soirée* of General D'Opotschinine, and I was beaten at chess by Count Litta.

1838. *April* 2.—Two hours of the morning (a remarkably bright one) were given to a stroll with Philip through the gallery of the Hermitage. I remarked more carefully than heretofore the paintings. The collections of Wouvermans, of Teniers, of Rembrandt, of Rubens, of Vandyke, and of Snyders, are each numerous and very fine, that of the last unrivalled. Several of Salvator Rosa, of Guido, and of Murillo are exquisite. The Raphaels are neither remarkable nor many. The Claude Lorrains and Carle Vernets are admirable. Some of Gerard Dow attracted a long gaze. Two mosaics, landscapes, more than a foot square, have all the richness, softness, and delicacy of the most finished paintings, and are the best things of the kind I ever saw. Some of Nicholas Poussin are of his highest excellence.

I noticed an immense painting, not hung but arranged on scaffolding, which was obviously the representation of a Review by the present Emperor at the head of a regiment of cuirassiers, either in Vienna or Berlin,—my ignorance of these two cities will not permit me to describe which, but I incline to the latter. The figures were all executed with the precision of miniatures, and were in number not less than two thousand. They are probably chiefly likenesses, that of the Emperor a striking one. The horses are done with inconceivable spirit. The group of fashionable spectators in the right corner of the picture is in itself a delightful study. I must ascertain the artist by inquiring this evening at Countess Laval's.

1838. *April* 7.—The day is kept by the Russians in a peculiar manner, and apparently for the especial benefit of children. The Gostenadvor has been surrounded by booths for vending toys and nicknackeries during the last three days, and the throng there to-day was great. Among other things bought and sold are switches of a shrub I could not recognize, seemingly just vegetating, and which are said to be accompanied in their use by good luck to the person flagellated.

1838. *April* 16.—Agreeably to the notice from the Grand Master of Ceremonies, I attended the Imperial Court at the palace of the Hermitage this morning at noon. The assembly was by no means as brilliant as the one at the beginning of the new year. The Diplomatic Corps were all present, except Count Schimmelpenninck, who absented himself in consequence of the scarlet-fever having raged in his family. The Empress was peculiarly splendid, having on a blue velvet tiara glistening with immense diamonds in the shape of ears of wheat, and a train of cloth of gold, deeply bordered with ermine. She wore also a broad, blue ribbon, emblematic of some order. Among the maids of honour I particularly noticed Marie de Benkendorff and Miss Lanskoy. The three Grand Duchesses, Marie, Olga, and Alexandrina, looked exceedingly pale, owing probably to their protracted fast. So did the Heir Apparent. A company of soldiers were ranged in one entry, all of whom were at least seven feet high. The Emperor informed me that he would travel into the central part of Europe in the course of a month or six weeks, " to take the waters for the benefit of his old years and of his old woman."

1838. *April* 20.—A stranger who has not witnessed can scarcely imagine the ardour with which the lower classes of this city give themselves during the present week, immediately following the long Caréme, to the most childish sports. They are encouraged, too, by all sorts of military and police arrangements. During the last three days of the week, and particularly in the afternoon, immense crowds collect at the common rendezvous in the square fronting the Admiralty, where have been erected temporary playhouses, circus, jugglers' booths, menageries, whirligigs of all kinds, flying-horses, swings, etc. During this afternoon, I should suppose there assembled no fewer than fifty or sixty thousand people, and the whole machinery of amusement was in full exercise. The throng of carriages, whose circuits are carefully directed and supervised by mounted dragoons, and whose multitudes and equipments are equally countless and showy, all in regular and unceasing motion, give to the *coup d'œil* the effect of a most magnificent panorama. The pervading silence forms, however, a forcible and eloquent contrast to the noise and bustle which would accompany such a scene in the United States. Scarcely anything is heard but the sound of the driving carriages, the bands of music within the theatres, or an occasional wild and monotonous song from the women who are swinging with great velocity. Real and loud hilarity is not discernible; nor, indeed, is it possible to find in any part of this dense mass the slightest disposition to quarrel or controversy; the great occupation of those who meet seeming to be, notwithstanding beards, moustaches, whiskers, and dirt, to exchange kisses on each side of the mouth.

1838. *April* 22.—The exhibition before the Admiralty has been eminently showy and amusing to-day, the last of the Carnival. I went with Philip on foot, while the ladies crowded the carriage. The multitude exceeded any assemblage I ever before saw; men, women, and children, all dressed with cleanliness and finery, and carriages without numbers, most of which were splendid equipages with four horses and gaudy liveries. Without the slightest tincture of exaggeration, I should say that there were collected not less than two hundred thousand human beings. The usual perfect order prevailed. The carriages, which moved in several regular lines in front of the space appropriated to diversions, were divided into as many concentric circles, and proceeded in a walk; had they formed in one straight line they must have extended seven or eight miles. At about half-past five, when I stood on the terrace of the Admiralty admiring the spectacle, I noticed the composed and slow progress of a high military officer on horseback, in what might be termed the centre aisle between the rows of carriages; he was distinguished by a broad blue ribbon, and was soon joined by another, whom I recognized as the Prince of Oldenburg. There was obviously now some ceremony preparing, and I waited for it. In a short time the Emperor, in a brilliant uniform of scarlet and white, mounted on a fine bay charger, appeared at one extremity of the aisle, accompanied by the Grand Duke Michel in a hussar uniform, and the Czarovitz in scarlet and white, with a throng of about a hundred aides-de-camp in the same glowing dress; the cavalcade passed up to the right extremity at which the Emperor formed it in a line. The Empress then, with her daughters, in an open barouche drawn by six grays, with three postilions clothed like jockeys in white satin jackets with light-blue satin sleeves and white breeches, and with silk cap and tassel, drove into the aisle and passed in front of his Majesty, by whom she was formally saluted; several carriages followed her with her maids of honour, and a crowd of officers attended. The glittering of the uniforms, the nodding of plumes, the richness of the equipages, the caracoling of the beautiful horses, and all combined with the immensity of the crowd, and its universal devotion to amusement and hilarity, produced an effect altogether beyond description. The Imperial Cortège rode up and down in the manner I have described several times.

I met the Emperor this morning on the English Quay. He was alone, stopped, shook me cordially by the hand, and after a little chat, informed me that he had received news from Lake Ladoga which rendered it probable that the ice in the Neva would break away in the course of two or three days. The weather indeed has been quite warm, and the wind southerly.

1838. *April* 25.—I visited Mr. Leiberman, the Prussian Minister, who entertained me with an active and ardent conversation on the expensiveness of living in St. Petersburg, and its real cause,—a system of monopoly and commercial restriction to which the Government so inflexibly adheres. He described the system of smuggling carried on upon the Prussion frontier here as constant and organized, and as continually leading to the most bloody conflicts between the borderers of the nations.

1838. *April* 26.—Bets on the departure of the ice in the Neva are numerous and heavy. The Emperor himself gambles on this event. It has been expected to move for several days, but remains firm; and one unacquainted, as I am, with the effects and operation by which it is secretly governed, would deem it stationary for ten days or two weeks more under almost any condition of atmosphere.

1838. *April* 27.—The ball at Count Braniska's was very brilliant, and attended by all the Imperial family. We went at eight and got home again at half-past one. Some of the apartments are beautiful; those appropriated to dancing and supping could not be surpassed. The service of gold on the table at which the Empress sat—a table that accommodated about twenty persons—was exquisite in its splendour and workmanship.

1838. *April* 28.—The ice in the Neva gave way and started on its downward course at about ten o'clock to-day. At about five in the afternoon, the usual ceremony was performed by the Emperor drinking a tumbler of the water, filling the tumbler with pieces of gold for the benefit of the officer who handed it, and ordering him to cross the river in his barge; the barge proceeds, cannon are fired when it is half-way, and again when over, and thenceforward the people are at liberty to use their wherries. The intercourse to-day between the city and the islands was suspended for about eight hours; between six and seven P.M. but few cakes of ice were perceptible. The bridge of boats was swung on one side at about noon, and will probably not be restored before to-morrow morning. I yesterday received a notice from the Grand Master of Ceremonies of an intention on the part of the Imperial Court to meet at the Hermitage on Sunday (to-morrow) at twelve, in celebration of the birthday of the Czarovitz, who is just twenty; but the notice has been to-day countermanded by a note from the same source, without assigning any reason.

1838. *April* 29.—The weather was delightfully mild. The river, entirely free from ice, was again thronged with the fanciful summer boats. We walked for an hour in the summer gardens, which were crowded with fashionable visitors.

1838. *May* 2.—Phil and I strolled towards the Champ-de-Mars, and had the good luck to meet there, in grand review and exercise, a body of about fifteen or twenty thousand cavalry. The Grand Duke Michel was present in command. Large squadrons went through the operation of charging at full gallop. The flying artillery was particularly interesting and exceedingly neat. This splendid exhibition was unaccompanied by the slightest noise or curiosity on the part of the population of the city. Perhaps it is too common to attract them; but matters of the sort are all arranged in secret; no newspapers advertise them; and after many inquiries, I have found it impossible to get to know when they take place.

1838. *May* 3.—This being a Court fête in honour of the births of the Empress and the Grand Duchess Alexandra, I attended at the palace of the Hermitage agreeably to notice at twelve o'clock. The presentation was in all respects very brilliant. In the evening at eight o'clock we repaired to a Court ball at the same palace.

1838. *May* 5.—The Emperor reviewed sixty thousand of his troops in the Champ-de-Mars at twelve o'clock to-day. We had obtained, through the kindness of General Ovander, accommodations in the military barracks fronting the scene, and commanded a complete view of the whole spectacle. Nothing could be finer; we went there at about half-past nine o'clock, and were early enough to witness the earliest preparations and every successive arrival of force. The parade-ground is a square in a level field of about fifty acres, whose surface is made earth, and which they were engaged with hoses and engines in watering so as effectually to lay the dust. By half-past eleven o'clock all the troops occupied their stations, and a large body could not be arranged on the field, but remained between it and the Great Quay. The proportions I should estimate thus, say forty-five thousand infantry and fifteen thousand cavalry and light artillery. Their equipments were all in the finest possible order : the brass cannon, the cuirasses, the muskets, and the front ornaments of the caps glittered dazzlingly in the sun. The horses, which in every regiment were of uniform colour, all of jet black or gray or sorrel or chocolate or bay, were beautiful without exception, and constituted perhaps the most striking feature of the exhibition; every officer was mounted on a charger equally spirited, graceful, and docile; the dresses of the various corps and squadrons were showy and effective. The Emperor came on the ground accompanied by a numerous staff, among whom were several military members of the diplomatic corps—Count Ficquelmont, Baron Palmstjerna, and Baron Seebach—a little after twelve o'clock, and cantered along the several fronts, saluted by a hurrah from every successive regiment, which he reciprocated by touching his hat. His progress awoke some fine music from the different bands. When he had finished, the Empress in an open landau with her three daughters, drawn by four bays with two postilions, reviewed the army in the same way. The two sovereigns then stationed themselves with their suite at the centre of one side of the square and the troops marched by before them. His Majesty was so much gratified by the manner with which the soldiers performed their duty that he ordered two roubles to be paid to each man. The precision and neatness of their movements well deserved this mark of approbation.

1838. *May* 7.—We started at half-past eight this morning, accompanied by the Marquis De Carréga and the Chevalier De Cossati, to visit the manufactories of glass and of porcelain, and the great cotton, hemp, and card factories at Alexandrofsky. The first we had visited on the 31st of March last, and were only additionally pleased by finding the workmen all at duty. Their number is four hundred. We failed to see a large mirror cast, but were gratified by seeing the simple process of putting the quicksilver upon the glass, and the still simpler one of making tubes for thermometers. The porcelain factory was at rest, all hands at dinner, and we only witnessed the machinery, the models, and some splendid specimens of the art in the "magazin;" a small dessert set of plates with admirable likenesses of eminent Russian officers were for sale at the price of one hundred and fifty roubles per plate. The chief exploit of the jaunt, however, was the exploring of the extensive Alexandrofsky factories, which enjoy great repute. They are ten versts or seven miles from the city, and constitute a most imposing collection of lofty buildings. They employ about three thousand hands, male and female, young and old. A large proportion of these are free artisans; the rest are called "children of the crown," and have been drawn from the foundling hospitals. The entire establishment has for many years been under the control of an Englishman, General Wilson, whose second in command is his brother; both were attentive to us. Several pieces of machinery were strikingly good; two steam-engines, one of one hundred and ten horse-power, and another of seventy; a novel process of carding wool, being two large wheels armed with several rows of long steel teeth bending somewhat from the circumference inwards and meeting in their revolutions so as to feed each other. This apparatus was introduced from England about eight years ago, and performs the task which would otherwise occupy thirty-one persons; the machinery for making playing-cards, printing, colouring, polishing, and cutting them, was exceedingly neat; as was also that for making sail-cloth and sheeting. We attended while six hundred of the operators took their dinner in a single wide and commodious apartment. Of these two hundred and seventeen were females, all clothed with great tidiness and seated all at one long table;—not a redeeming ray of beauty in the whole assemblage. The fare was good: corn-beef, soup, millet, and black bread; no vegetables. The dinner was preceded and closed with a short hymn decently sung; and every movement of entrance or departure was characterized by the formality, precision, and silence of military discipline. Not a word was uttered during the repast. The Chapel is handsome,—its walls and ceiling washed with light blue and studded with golden stars, and it is capable of containing all the tenants of the factory. Roomy accommodations are devoted to recreation and to schooling. The bedrooms are remarkably airy and cleanly. One noble hall is reserved for occasions of exhibition before the Imperial patrons. All the range of structure is fire-proof; the ceilings are arched with cast-iron, the staircases are of stone or iron, and the roofs are either tile or iron. We were detained so long in making the above visits that we did not get home until half-past two, and I lost the opportunity of attending, according to engagement, at the new Church of St. Isaac, in order to witness the raising of one of the immense pillars of granite which are to sustain the great dome.

1838. *May* 8.—A strong northwesterly wind has brought down the ice from Lake Ladoga. The river is crowded with it. The cold has become unpleasant in consequence, and snow has fallen. As this is the largest lake in Europe, having a superficies of more than six thousand square miles, and no outlet for its ice but the Neva, we must expect the chilling current to continue for some days. The southwestern extremity of Ladoga is about thirty miles east of St. Petersburg.

Notwithstanding the obvious danger of crossing the river while this vast field of ice is driving, the wherries are plying with great activity and much crowded. The bridge is necessarily swung on one side, and all communication cut off except by the boats. Many are taken by surprise, and compelled by the urgency of business to incur the risk. This afternoon a flat-bottomed wherry, loaded with seven persons, upset amid the ice, and all hands perished.

1838. *May* 10.—Yesterday the river was sufficiently clear of ice to permit the reinstatement of the bridge; to-day, however, a new arrival has cut off the communication. No passage open yet for navigation between this and Cronstadt. Our days are becoming long. It was a clear and rich twilight when we returned from Mrs. Gillebrand's.

1838. *May* 13.—This being first of May, Old Style, is usually signalized by a sort of gay fête at Katarinoff, about three miles out of town, when a procession of equipages, headed by some members of the Imperial family, go thither, " to meet the Spring," and to parade in lines around a sort of garden or open park in which the multitude are amusing themselves in their own way. We drove out, found it dull and the weather bad, and were wholly disappointed.

The Emperor and Czarovitz quit for Berlin this morning.

1838. *May* 17.—The ice, in considerable quantities, is again drifting down the river, but the weather is exceedingly pleasant. The Gulf of Finland, below Cronstadt, for seventy or eighty versts, is yet an unbroken sheet of ice. Vessels are said to be in sight waiting for an opening.

Mrs. Cramer's last dance for the season was attended by all of us. We went at 9.30 in daylight, and returned at 2.30 in the morning and broad day.

The last of the twenty-four granite pillars on the top and exterior of the dome of St. Isaac's Church was placed on Monday last. This completes an undertaking of considerable skill and hazard. Each of these columns is forty-two feet in length, four feet nine inches in breadth at the base, and weighs one hundred and sixty thousand pounds. The arch on which they rest is one hundred and sixty feet above the floor of the church. This church will be adorned in its various parts with not less than one hundred and four of these granite columns, whose combined weight is estimated at eleven million one hundred and fifty-six thousand pounds. The highest point of the edifice, when finished, will be at an elevation of three hundred and twenty-nine feet. I have marked, almost daily, the operation of raising these columns. Not the slightest noise, accident, or confusion occurred at any time, although the work was sometimes going on when Réaumur stood at 10°.

1838. *May* 18.—The ice, early this morning, came down the river in large quantities. It interrupts the intercourse with Vassili-Ostroff seriously. Rumor states that two Baltic steamers are in the Gulf of Finland, prevented by the ice from reaching Cronstadt.

The Austrian Ambassador, Count Ficquelmont, called to take leave, intending to quit here with his wife tomorrow morning. He returns, he says, in November: the Countess will remain in a milder climate for eighteen months.

The Emperor did not leave Sarsko-Selo until it turned Tuesday morning last: this owing to the universal Russian superstition against commencing a journey on Monday. He delayed his departure till a half-hour after midnight, and then started full gallop.

1838. *May* 19.—Agreeably to arrangement we proceeded, at eleven o'clock, to visit the Corps of Marine Cadets, situated on the quay on Vassili-Ostroff, and superintended by the celebrated navigator, Admiral Adam John de Krusenstern, who performed the voyage around the globe in 1803–1806. His invitation had been exceedingly kind, and we resolved to be punctual. As the bridge was not yet replaced, owing to the floating ice, we occupied two wherries, being accompanied by Mr. Cossato and Mr. Chew, and by three servants, and were rowed over rapidly. The Admiral and his two daughters received us, and we were regaled immediately with hot chocolate. He would seem to be about seventy-three or -five years of age, resembles in countenance and figure, very strongly, our former President Monroe, and is remarkably unaffected and benevolent in his manner. While we were sipping chocolate, he drew my attention to two Chinese paintings which had been sent to him, representing the Emperor of China seated in state, with his great officers about him and ready to give audience. He had received them *via* New York, and believed them the only specimens of Chinese art of that description which had reached Europe. I could only think them curious. The next two hours were wholly occupied in examining the noble institution, of which, after having been the second Governor during a short period of eight months, he has now been the chief for more than twelve years. He led us into all the interesting departments excepting the Observatory, which he said was too lofty to be reached by the ladies without great fatigue; and he explained everything as he went along with a simplicity and interest which heightened our gratification. The building is an immense quadrangle, whose front on the river may be about eight hundred feet. It accommodates six hundred pupils, with all the necessary teachers, the retinue of servants, the Admiral's family, countless apartments appropriated to museums, libraries, reception-rooms, models, moulding, etc., and four large open lots for recreation and sport. None are admitted into this Imperial institution except the sons of noblemen; one hundred of them pay for their own tuition, at the rate of one hundred and fifty roubles, or one hundred and twenty-five dollars per annum, and for that sum, in addition to instruction, are found in everything,—boarding, lodging, clothing, books, and a suit of uniform when they quit; the other five hundred of them are paid for by the Emperor. The regular course lasts six years, and at the close the pupil is an officer in the navy, and enters active service. About eighty are thus ushered into the world every year. Nothing would seem to be spared in labour and expense in order to make their training perfect. The Emperor has devoted three beautiful small frigates exclusively to their use, in which they are constantly practising, during the summer season, in the bay between this and Cronstadt. Every class has, in its turn, ample opportunity for this practical experience. But in the building itself, for the special initiation of the younger classes, there has been constructed a small man-of-war brig, furnished with all the spars and ropes, and strong enough as well as roomy enough to permit a crew of twenty to go through all the exercises of making sail, tacking, taking in, etc. We were delighted at witnessing this at full play under the orders of a lad of great promise, about fifteen years of age, the son of an acquaintance, Princess Gallitzin. In the same vast apartment, at one end of it, has been stationed what is denominated the dock-yard, in which there is building a seventy-four, every timber and plank of which is fitted with screws, so as to be capable of being taken to pieces and of being rebuilt by each successive class. The keel is fifty-seven feet in length, and the beam is fourteen. This admirable structure originated with Krusenstern, and he proposes by it to give to every one of his students an ample knowledge of every part of a vesssel of war, of the relation of all the parts, and of ship-building generally. Near this, also, were erected two sections of a man-of-war's bulwarks, each with a port-hole, one with a long gun, the other with a carronade, both of brass, fitted to practise the levelling, taking sight, loading, and firing. The same apartment, of whose vast dimensions I forget the particulars, is used as a refectory; and we were highly gratified by seeing the entire corps of six hundred drummed to their dinner in exact order. The astronomical apparatus, the models of a number of celebrated ships, and the engraving of a remarkable sea-fight, were all interesting. The capital library, too, stored with volumes in various languages, was superintended by an officer decorated with an order of merit. The dormitories were airy and extensive; the apartments for the sick were unexceptionable, and here we saw a recent English invention of a bed made of water,—in other words, a mattress of gum-elastic filled with that fluid,—which the Admiral assured us had been found, on trial, the easiest bed for the invalid. The kitchen appeared commodious and ample. One pervading quality struck us all in relation to the whole institution,—its extreme neatness and cleanliness, the total absence, even in the hospital and kitchen, of the slightest offensive appearance or odour. While walking through the museum, I remarked two pieces of fanciful carving in black wax,—one a troika, of small size,—and was told by the Admiral that they were the untaught and unaided productions of one of his pupils; that the boy had manifested no particular capacity for the naval service, but had suddenly exhibited this sort of talent and taste, and that about five days ago the Emperor, who is very fond of the establishment, paid it a visit before going to Berlin, and, noticing the two specimens on the table, inquired about their author, and immediately directed that he should be sent, under his particular auspices, to be instructed in the Academy of Arts. The Admiral and his two daughters politely escorted us to the wharf at a little after one o'clock, and we agreed in the opinion that our morning had been most agreeably and advantageously spent.

At two o'clock we drove to the Hermitage, expecting to treat ourselves and the young ones with hearing the far-famed golden peacock, golden cock, and golden owl, under a golden tree, on a golden grass-plat, surrounded by enormous precious stones, make their respective peculiar noises of screaming, crowing, and hooting. The machinery, however, was out of repair, and we had to content ourselves with astonishing the eyes without the ears. Finding Mr. Labensky present, I ascertained from him that the painter of the magnificent and interesting picture I had noticed on a former visit—the Review in Berlin—is named Cruger, and is a native of that city. All its remarkable personages are miniature likenesses; and he pointed out to me in the right corner of the picture two figures of no little celebrity in a sort of dearborn or open carriage,—Paganini seated, and Sontag (now Countess Rossi) standing alongside of him. He showed me also Baron Humboldt in the crowd.

1838. *May* 20.—Being the anniversary of our sailing out of the harbour of Boston on board the Independence, we were visited by a young gentleman of that city, Mr. Sumner, just arrived, and the first who reached Cronstadt through the ice this season in a Charleston brig, The Hardy, who was present and saw us take our departure in our noble frigate.

1838. *June* 3.—We spent the evening at Countess Nesselrode's, not returning home until half-past twelve, at which hour the twilight was so beautiful and clear that I was able to read distinctly in crossing St. Isaac's Square. I met at Nesselrode's for the first time the celebrated Speranski, who, under Alexander, systemized the laws, gave offence to the boyars, fell into disgrace, and was some time in Siberia. His head and entire figure—a tall, slim, bald-headed man in black—reminded me strongly of Mr. Robert M. Taylor, of Philadelphia. Count Nesselrode leaves here for Berlin on Tuesday next.

1838. *June* 7.—The son of Baron Steiglitz called while I was yet at breakfast to inform me of what had just occurred at Mrs. Wilson's boarding-house. A young Bostonian, recently arrived, by the name of Hall had attempted to destroy himself by cutting his throat with a razor; he inflicted some deep gashes, but failed to effect his purpose. Information of the fact having been sent to the police, its agents were in attendance, and were about removing him to an Imperial hospital. I immediately went over and visited the unfortunate man. He was lying in bed on his back; the wounds had been sewed up and bandaged; he had bled profusely, but the redness of his face indicated considerable fever; the officers of police were engaged in drafting a *procès-verbal*, and had their surgeon with them. Several American captains were present,—Captain Dwyer, Captain Trask. I immediately inquired into the nature of the wounds, the ability of the man to bear removal, the character of the hospital, and the manner in which he would probably be treated, etc. He was himself anxious to be sent, and the physicians and all his companions thought he would be far better off if he went to the hospital. Mrs. Wilson, too, said it was impossible for her to have him properly nursed at her house. On the whole, I thought the removal the only step that could be taken to secure his life, especially as the police-officer assured me that he should be vigilantly guarded against the paroxysm of fever and be most carefully attended. He was taken to the hospital about two o'clock. Mr. Chew went there at four in order to see that all was right.

1838. *June* 8.—Mr. Chew reports that poor Hall is quite contented with his accommodations and is promising very well.

1838. *June* 15.—Attended the funeral service of Rodofinikine at the Monastery of St. Alexander Nefsky. It lasted for nearly three hours. The number of officiating priests was about twelve, of whom two appeared of high rank by the richness of their tiaras and vestments, and by the deference with which they were treated. The ceremonies were excessively monotonous and tiresome, seeming to involve much of superstition and much of image reverence. The kissing the hands, the garments, and the feet of certain of the priests was incessant; and the pictures of saints, the book of prayer, and even the tables and their carpeting underwent the same frequent endearment. A dirge was admirably sung by a numerous choir without any instrumental music. One voice, that of an active officiating priest, indicated prodigious power, and transcended even that of Angrisani. The body lay in state under a gorgeous canopy of crimson velvet and gold surmounted with crimson and white plumes. The coffin, which rested on a platform raised four or five feet by steps from the floor, was of rich scarlet cloth worked with gold and edged with gold lace; its seam was marked by double rows of white lace two or three inches deep. During the ceremonies a heavy drapery of cloth of gold covered the lower part of the coffin, which was removed, when the coffin was taken to a side door, opened, and earth thrown upon the body. During a portion of the time every person present held a wax taper, and before the coffin was moved the kindred and servants of the deceased went up the steps and kissed it. It is unfair to form or express an opinion as to ceremonies of this sort, without understanding the meaning of their various parts; it certainly did not appear to produce the slightest appropriate impression upon any who witnessed it. The deceased was furnished with a *passport* and a *dish of rice pudding!*

1838. *June* 16.—The Imperial standard unexpectedly waves over the palace of Anischoff. His Majesty has taken his good city by surprise; it is said also that he returns from an abrupt incog. visit to Stockholm, where he remained but a few hours.

1838. *June* 19.—Having procured from Count Cancrin an introductory note, we all went at one o'clock to visit the Mint and Church within the Fortress opposite the Marble Palace.

The church is exceedingly rich in its interior decorations; the altar-piece and ornaments being either of gold or splendidly worked and gilded. Its walls are almost lined with standards taken during the wars of Alexander. The tombs of the Emperors and Empresses, in number eight or ten, are stationed on the floor in different parts of the church; that of Alexander looks almost as ancient as that of Peter; they are of uniform size and height, oblong squares of granite or marble slabs about three feet high and six feet long; they are first covered with cloth of gold bordered with ermine, and then again with a woollen covering on which the initials of the deceased are worked; medals were fastened on the top; and two keys, one immense, probably of surrendered fortresses, lay on the tomb of Alexander. The steeple of this is celebrated for its golden covering, which to-day, as the sun was clear, shone too dazzlingly to be looked at.

The Mint was interesting in all its details. The quantities of Siberian gold and silver collected in immense bars and huge square cakes exceeded expectation. We were furnished an English guide, who accompanied us throughout the establishment and explained the various processes that were in operation, by which the two metals were purified of each other, and, finally, stamped into coin. The machinery appeared to be extensive and admirable. In the department appropriated to medals we were gratified by being shown a series commemorative of the incidents of Alexander's reign, designed and executed by Count Tolstoi, himself the best die-sinker in the country. The reverse of every medal was the bust of the Emperor as Achilles.

In a separate building we found, carefully preserved, the large boat alleged to have been constructed by Peter the Great himself.

1838. *June* 29.—Went to the Alexandrofsky Theatre, in the Nefsky, fronting on the square between the Imperial Library and the palace of Anischoff. This and the Great Theatre are two of the finest probably in the world. There are six tiers of boxes. The decorations and police are imperial throughout. The performances of this evening were in Russian, and, of course, unintelligible to us; but we could perceive that one of them was a lively and ludicrous farce, descriptive of the sensation produced here by the appearance of Taglioni and of the press for admission to her representations.

1838. *July* 3.—The revolt of Stockholm, consequent upon the punishment of a newspaper editor for some remark as to the manner in which the Emperor was treated on his last visit, appears to have been a serious affair; to have continued with various excesses for some days, and to have been accompanied with the loss of many lives. The last accounts leave the affair unfinished, and the artillery arrayed against the people.

1838. *July* 6.—Mr. Daschkoff accompanied us this afternoon on a ride in search of a country-seat. We went across the islands to the mainland and visited a church recently built, which owed its structure to circumstances of considerable interest. It is exceedingly pretty, and has just been erected by a rich noble lady of the name of Vassiltevich, the altar being placed on the very spot where her only son breathed his last. This young man, it appears, became enamoured of a female somewhat inferior to him in social position, and his mother inflexibly opposed the union. They were kept apart for some years, until, owing to one cause or another, he declined further intercourse with her; her brother challenged him; they met two or three hundred yards from the spot on which the church stands, fired at about fifteen paces' distance, and both shots were fatal. Vassiltevich was carried to an inn which stood on the present site of the church, and shortly afterwards expired. His antagonist died on the field. The place of the duel is in a garden with trees and shrubbery around, and the precise spot of each combatant is marked by a flat, round block of granite about three feet in diameter and one foot high. The mother, whose wealth is boundless, actuated for some time by extreme hatred of the family of her son's destroyer, resolved to purchase the whole scene of action, to convert the battle-ground into promenade gardens, with the granite mementos mentioned, and to construct a church at which every prayer that was uttered should be accompanied by a curse upon the soul and family of her son's enemy. The priests interfered, and, after several years of persuasion, induced her to abandon the last part of her design, and, as both the young men had died without absolutions, to dedicate the edifice to both as a proof of her Christian forgiveness. The columns, altar-pieces, and windows of stained glass, now in all their freshness, are very beautiful. It is called the Church of St. Vladimar.

1838. *July* 13.—We visited to-day the encampment near the village of Krasno-Celo. The distance is exactly twenty-four versts, or, say, sixteen miles. We started with two carriages and four at half-past nine, and reached the village at eleven o'clock, and returned to a late dinner at six. The camp, which is regularly opened as soon as the summer begins, and is said to contain a force of about forty thousand, spreads itself on the heights to the east of the town, and in the form of a horseshoe extends about two miles. It is beautifully laid out. We drove through some of its principal sections. As it is the birthday of the Empress, the soldiers were engaged in saying mass around the chapel of their respective quarters, and the solemn silence which prevailed while the thousands stood uncovered was exceedingly exemplary and impressive. The tents were all in the finest order of arrangement and cleanliness. The *coup d'œil* from the village was peculiarly fine.

At ten o'clock to-night we ordered the carriage and drove to Kamenoi-Ostroff to witness a succession of fireworks prepared by the Princess Beloselsky in honor of the day. The crowd exceeded anything I ever beheld, covering the land and water as far as the eye could pierce, and forming, from the boats to the highest points of Hilagon near the Imperial château, a vast and dense amphitheatre of human beings. There must have been more than two hundred thousand present. The fireworks were arranged on the Christofsky beach, in front of the Beloselsky palace, and on the broad and smooth arm of the Neva, which divided Christofsky and Hilagon. The position was admirably chosen, and permitted every one of the countless crowd to enjoy the entire exhibition. The brilliancy of the rockets, of the various *feux de joie*, of the revolving lights, and of the illuminated temples and pavilions, on the principal of which the name of Alexandra in capitals of fire was vividly conspicuous, exceeded expectations.

1838. *July* 19.—Visited the Academy of Fine Arts, accompanied by Mrs. Dallas and my daughters. The collection of casts is remarkably fine, some of them of modern subjects. Devoted exclusively to the cultivation and encouragement of native talent, the number of copies of celebrated paintings is large. An original one of great size has been placed in the Academy since my last visit, and purports to represent the arrival of the Grand Duchess Helen, after her marriage, at the Champ-de-Mars. Her likeness, in a coach drawn by eight horses, is strikingly good; the front of the canvas is crowded with admirable miniatures of the distinguished persons, military and civil, who participated in the ceremony of the reception. The Emperor, on horseback, attended by a group, at the head of which appears the young Czarovitz, and the Ambassador of Austria, Count Ficquelmont, are faithfully delineated. The immense picture representing the Emperor mounted on his bay charger, and in full military costume, whence the best engraved likenesses are taken, improved upon further inspection; the other figures are: nearest the Emperor on his left, the Czarovitz; behind the Czarovitz, Count Cernicheff, the Minister of War; nearest the Emperor on his right, though a little in the rear, is Volkonsky; next and prominent is the Grand Duke Michel; next retreating is Count Benkendorff; and farthest, but forward, is Paskevitch, Prince of Warsaw. The vast painting delineating the destruction of Pompeii attracted Mrs. Dallas's admiration; its colours, however, are too glowing for my taste.

1838. *July* 26.—Spent the day at Pavlovsky, agreeably to the invitation of Countess Schimmelpenninck. Our time was made very pleasant by rides through the Imperial Park, and by visits to the monuments erected by the late Empress's mother, Marie,—one to her own parents, the King and Queen of Würtemberg, and the other to her husband Paul. The latter monument is remarkably beautiful and in fine taste; it is contained in a small Doric temple with colonnade of red granite columns in front, covering a large door of ornamented iron railing, directly opposite to which is the tomb. The tomb is composed of immense slabs of red porphyry, shaped pyramidally; near the apex is a fine medallion of white marble, being an admirable head of the deceased Emperor; and below it on a platform of porphyry, weeping at an urn, is an exquisitely chiselled female figure, on her knees and bending forward, representing the widowed Empress; in front and below the platform is a large bass-relief of white marble representing all the children,—Alexander seated on the right, clothed in armor, with casque off, in an ecstasy of grief, covering his face with his hands, while Constantine, Nicholas, and Michel approach to console him; the young sisters are also drawing near; two of the elder ones, married, are mournfully retiring; an infant in a cloud, early deceased, beckons the figure of another sister who also died. The whole work is exceedingly neat and in capital preservation. It is placed in a very retired and silent part of the Park. We visited also the palace of the Pavilion of Roses. The palace was built by the

Empress Marie, and became her permanent residence after Paul's death. It has been religiously kept in the precise condition in which she left it, by the present Grand Duke Michel, who alleges that he cannot bear to live in a house which reminds him at every corner of his early happiness and of a parent whom he adored, and who resides in a comparatively wretched building at some distance from the palace. His true reason is the known lack of funds to renovate and modernize. The furniture is costly and beautiful, but not in the reigning fashion. Its tapestry is beautiful. Some of the paintings are very fine. The library is the precious apartment, and is much resorted to. The hall of reception is a vast square. Several of the cabinets were hung with the drawings, paintings, and plaster modellings of the Empress, whose sentiment was strongly displayed in the groupings of her children. As soon as I entered one of the rooms, I remembered instantly to have been in it before, though until that moment it had escaped my recollection; it was the apartment in which twenty-five years ago I had been presented to the Empress mother. We returned home by the railroad at half-past eleven o'clock, having exceedingly enjoyed our excursion.

1838. *July* 28.—On the invitation of the Marquis Carrega, I visited the Winter Palace, in order to see the progress of the building. We were accompanied by one of the superintendents. There is a wilderness of scaffolding and a world of rubbish. Nothing intimates that the work can be thoroughly accomplished short of five or six years. The southern section may possibly be fitted up by next April, so as to admit the Imperial family. There are three thousand men employed on the building.

1838. *July* 29.—Started at four P.M., and reached the country-seat of Mr. S. Cramer near the village and on the river Ochta at five, where we dined and remained until half-past nine. We were saluted by the American flag, which floated during our stay. The place is esteemed the handsomest of which the environs can boast, and is said to have been built by the celebrated Potemkin. It is exceedingly showy in the style and structure of its apartments, and, though built of brick, seems fitted for fine and warm weather only. Mrs. Cramer has recently sold it to General Zerkazanet for two hundred and fifty thousand roubles, a price which must appear very low when it is remembered that it is but about seven miles from the city, easily accessible, and embraces about three thousand acres of land, two splendid dwelling-houses, and eighty male serfs with their families and villages. We here met the brother of Mr. Bodisco who is Russian Minister at Washington and a colonel in the Russian army.

1838. *August* 1.—At nine this morning we went to Cronstadt on board the steamboat, performing the passage in about two hours. Our Consul, Mr. Lenartzen, apprised of our intention to come, had informed the Government, and everything that could contribute to our comfort and amusement was prepared. The Governor's aid, Colonel Romanoff, with the Consul and his eldest daughter, met us at the wharf, and after the other passengers had landed, the steamboat was directed to take us on board the Admiral's frigate, the Aurora, lying at a distance. A barge of fourteen oars was also ready and taken in tow. The Aurora is a showy ship of in fact sixty guns, the upper-deck carronades, with a crew of four hundred men, four lieutenants and six midshipmen.

Great neatness and cleanliness were conspicuous; but the seamen were kept out of sight. An apparatus was shown me by the captain, which he said had been in use for five years back,—an immense air-pump which changed the atmosphere of every part of the ship below with great rapidity; the draught in its funnels, while the machine was in operation, was so great as to blow out one's handkerchief when put in. On leaving the Aurora to return to the steamboat, a salute was fired of thirteen guns. Having landed, we took to our barge and proceeded to visit the immense new dry-dock, now rapidly completing. The work is truly an imperial one,—executed of fine granite and adapted to accommodate a ship of one hundred and twenty guns. The masonry is beautiful. The builder, General Foulon, was present, and his assistant, of the name of Wilson, exhibited and explained the drafts of the work. With the aid of an immense reservoir or well and steam enginery attached, it is computed that the dock may be emptied, after the ship is once floated in and fixed, in the course of thirty-six hours. There are a long range of other dry-docks, and these we saw to great advantage, crowded with a number of ships of the line undergoing all sorts of repairs. At the head of one of the docks, in a small building exclusively appropriated to it, we were shown a model of the entire island of Cronstadt and its harbour and adjacent castles and forts. This model consists of a sort of immense table of great solidity, on the smooth surface of which have been placed small wooden houses and other buildings indicating with the minutest accuracy every improvement. It presented to the eye exactly such a view as one might have of the island from a balloon two or three miles above it. We now quit our barge and proceeded in carriages to visit the arsenal and to ride around the walls. The veteran general in command at the arsenal, who received us in much state, accompanied by five or six of his aids, could not, unfortunately for us, speak any language but Russ, and our inquiries, passing necessarily through Colonel Romanoff or the Consul, were on that account limited. The collection of military material here was very great. On the first floor were arranged the carriages of a thousand cannon with all their adjuncts and equipments; on the upper floor, muskets, swords, pistols, swivels, pikes, and small-arms of every possible description, were arranged in countless quantities, and in a most tasteful manner, reminding us of the display we had witnessed at the Tower in London, and surpassing that in everything, except perhaps in the number of muskets. On the adjoining field was a splendid exhibition of five thousand pieces of ordnance, many of them of dazzling brass, of all calibres and sizes and shapes; and these were flanked by mounds of cannon-shot and shells, which exceeded in number sixteen thousand. This show of iron force transcended anything I have seen.

The singular and solid masonry of the walls, as we rode between them and the outer fosse, was well worth seeing; and it was impossible not to notice everywhere that the Government was expending immense sums of money in ornamenting the island. Numerous ranges of superb barracks are finishing; and brick parapets of great solidity are constructing. On one of the buildings a colonel of engineers seemed to take great pride in pointing out some inscriptions which indicated that three or four of the foundation-stones had been laid by the Emperor, Count Woronzow, Prince Volkonsky, etc. It is said that his Majesty annually appropriates four million roubles to the works of Cronstadt, for which he has long exhibited an unabated partiality, and which he says he will make a little St. Petersburg. It contains a permanent population exceeding ten thousand. The military force on the island equals twenty thousand. A fleet could not approach with hostile intentions without having a thousand cannon pointed at it from the numerous fortifications. Being cordially entertained at dinner by Mr. Leonartzen and his two daughters, we returned to the steamboat at six o'clock and reached home at nine.

1838. *August* 17.—We started at half-past twelve and reached Pergola, the country residence of Prince Butera, at about half-past two. The distance is about eighteen versts, or twelve miles, in a northwestern direction. The situation is the finest we have yet seen, as there is something like hill and dale. The estate, principally owned by the son of the Princess by her first husband, Count Shuvaloff, is extensive and highly improved. The display of dahlias and other rich flowers is very great. The conservatories are large and supply tropical and other fruits at all seasons; there are quantities of pineapples, peaches, nectarines, and grapes, ripening and ripe. The Princess, who has had the luck to have three husbands, erected to her second a handsome monument, which is surrounded by a small iron railing, preserved in undisturbed tranquillity, and decorated with flowers. The monument is enclosed in a tomb, sodded and planted, and the marble is only perceptible through the grating of the door. It is said that she placed alongside of her husband's an open tomb for herself, and that some malicious personage, since her present marriage, visiting it, wrote within "*for my next husband,*" since which access has been denied, and the spot preserved from intrusion. Her second husband had been the tutor of the children by her first, and is spoken of in terms of great praise by those who knew him. He purchased his title of Count, and when dying expressed a wish to be interred among the noblesse at the Church of St. Alexander Nefsky; but the Emperor Nicholas forbade it. Her eldest son, Count Shuvaloff, about nineteen or twenty, has recently returned from the wars in Circassia, where he received a wound in the breast. He is prepossessing, intelligent, and a very modest gentleman. The Princess has been building for some years back, and will now soon finish, a neat Gothic church on a hill within sight of the mansion. It is built of the soft stone found on her estate, which is yellowish with veins of blue, and has much the appearance of half-baked brick. We rambled in every direction through the park and other grounds enjoying the scenery and shrubbery and fresh air; we were regaled with a *déjeûner à la fourchette* immediately after arriving, with a dinner at half-past four, and with tea and fruits at half-past eight, while in the intervals we frolicked with the mimic ice-hills, the swings, seesaws, bagatelles, etc.; we reached home about half-past ten, delighted with our excursion.

1838. *August* 20.—I accompanied my daughters to Pavlovsky. We spent the day at Count Schimmelpenninck's, and did not reach home again until half-past eleven at night. In the course of conversation I learned that the Count had studied the law, intending to practise it; that the death of his father diverted him to commerce; that he became President of the Dutch East India Company; was Secretary of State by appointment of the present King, and is a member of the first or upper house of the States-General. He is of opinion that there exist several incurable defects in the existing constitution of Holland, which soon must produce its destruction; of these he referred particularly to the complicated process by which the members of the second or lower house of Legislature are chosen from the provinces, and the inability of the King, who alone originates and is responsible for laws, without the intervention of ministers to enforce his methods or to avoid unpopularity when resisted and assailed. The upper house, created by the King alone, is merely for life, and having no hold upon popular sentiment, and no support, as in England, from a permanent and organized order, is esteemed a mere useless agent of the monarch, and cannot, with any success, at any time or on any subject resist the popular branch. The Count's grandfather was Ambassador from Holland at Paris. His father was the last pensioner and became stone blind, and the family indulge a notion that Napoleon, in order to get rid of him and to prepare the way for his brother, Louis, had a poisonous powder enclosed in a complimentary letter to him, by which he was instantly deprived of sight. The Count says that the Princess of Orange has been travelling in Germany this summer incog. under the title of Countess *Van Buren.*

1838. *October* 8.—During the last two days the arrival of the Emperor with his whole family has been hourly expected on board his steamer, the Hercules, from Stettin. Preparations were made for their landing on the English Quay, and we have been kept on the *qui vive.* It is now ascertained that, having encountered a rough sea and the ladies suffering greatly, the whole party has landed on the coast and will travel hither by land.

I returned the visit of Admiral Krusenstern and left with him a newspaper from the United States, containing some paragraphs about our exploring expedition, in which he professes to take much interest. In the course of our conversation the Admiral likened the Circassians to our Cherokee and Creek Indians, and said that the frequency and cruelty of their incursions into Russia caused the present war, a war which Russia really felt no inclination to pursue, but was forced by a principle of self-preservation to aid.

I visited Barante, the French Ambassador, who arrived with his family on Saturday evening last. He was very cordial, spoke eloquently about his journey up the Mediterranean, to Greece, to Constantinople, to Odessa, to the Crimea, and through Russia to Moscow. He has been treated throughout in a manner extremely flattering and agreeable. He asked me what was thought in the United States of the French blockade of the Mexican coast. I told him that we entertained very little doubt about its justice, as we ourselves were sufferers from Mexican misconduct; but that we began to think that they were rather unnecessarily interfering with our commerce, and we did not think it quite compatible with the honour and glory of so powerful a nation to be attacking, for an amount of damages less than a million of dollars, so young, so weak, so poor, and so distracted a republic as Mexico. "Well, but," said he, "what can be done with a country which has scarcely anything that can be called a government? We have no other resource." I said we had referred our controversy with Mexico to umpirage when we were on the eve of war; he turned the conversation instantly, and told me he had just received the intelligence that the difficulty with Switzerland was at an end, that Louis Napoleon had quit that country. He intended that I should understand that the French cabinet had attained its object. I merely remarked that I had known some time ago that Louis Napoleon had obtained a passport for England, "but," said I, "was there not much false importance given to this business? Why exaggerate the consequence and fame and dangerous character of a man who is without abilities, and whose affair at Strasburg only made him ridiculous? In the United States such a person no one would ever dream of persecuting into importance; he would be allowed to sink by his own weight." "That is true," he remarked, "of the United States, where order is so well and has been so long established that no one entertains the slightest apprehension of disturbances arising from political ambition; but we in France have been kept in such a perpetual turmoil and suffering that we deem it the part of wisdom and prudence to take measures to crush or thwart everything of the sort as early as possible."

Horace Vernet's picture, finished this year for the Emperor, is now in the Hermitage. Philip and I visited it to-day. It represents Napoleon reviewing his Imperial guard in the Thuilleries, behind the palace, between it and the celebrated triumphal arch on which were placed the four bronzed Venetian horses. The hero is followed by an immense throng of marshals, aids, etc., splendidly mounted and equipped, while he himself, on a superb white charger, is characterized by great simplicity of dress, a plain cocked hat without feather or cockade, white smallclothes, and with a face and figure which do his character and achievements entire justice. It is the finest portraiture of the wonderful man I have yet seen. He is in the act of slightly checking his horse at an extremity of one of the lines, as he beholds an old wooden-legged soldier, whose wounds in the head are yet bandaged, and who stands between two of his boys, stretching towards him a written petition. Murat's steed is as noble an Arabian as the imagination can possibly shadow forth. He was the only one of the train of whose identity I could entertain no doubt. The perspective of the ranks of soldiers is admirably executed. As a painting, there is a boldness, spirit, correctness of colouring, and unity of design which cannot be surpassed.

1838. *October* 9.—The Imperial standard is hoisted on the Anischoff palace, his Majesty and all his family having reached Sarsko-Selo yesterday afternoon.

1838. *October* 19.—Escorted Mrs. Dallas to the Hermitage in order to show her Vernet's review. It grows finer and finer the more it is examined. Eugene Beauharnais is the splendid figure in green. In the same room, since my last visit, several delightful objects have been collected, no doubt lately purchased by the Emperor. The two pieces of sculpture, The Bacchante, by Bienaimé, and The Dying Psyche, by Tenerani, are exquisite: the former is inimitable. An Imperial review on the Champ-de-Mars, by a Russian artist, seems to be put there as a set-off to Cruger and Vernet. It is an equally large canvas, crowded with figures, among which the Emperor, Empress, Grand Duchess Marie, Grand Duke Michel, Czarovitz, Counts Orloff, Benkendorf, etc., are easily recognized, but the painting is comparatively wretched. Bienaimé's Bacchante is dated at Rome, 1838.

1838. *October* 22.—Went, accompanied by Madame Daschkoff, to the Russian theatre, and witnessed one act of the Gazza Ladra, and Taglioni again in the Maid of the Danube. The Emperor and Empress were present.

So were the Marquis and Marchioness Clanricarde, Baron and Baroness Barante, Count and Countess Rossi, etc. The Clanricardes promise very little. The Marquis is a tall, pale, and long-faced, bald and awkward-looking man with a repulsive physiognomy; and his wife, with marked features and fashionable air, would seem very much like a spoiled and dashing beauty whose colour had faded under the effect of a family of nine children.

1838. *November* 1.—I visited old Mr. Poletica this morning, and found him unwell from a severe cold which suddenly attacked him yesterday. He has spent, during the last summer, three weeks at Constantinople, probably to unite his efforts with those of other Russian diplomats in order to prevent, if possible, the recently announced treaty between Turkey and England, which would seem to remove the Sultan from under the control of the Czar, and to subject him to French and British influence, the latter guaranteeing to him the dependence of Mehemet Ali. Mr. Poletica remembers but little of our country; has, perhaps, never been its friend, and is wholly ignorant of the real character of its recent history. He meddled with more art and success than candour in formation of the treaty of 1824, by which Mr. Middleton has entailed upon the relations of Russia and America an embarrassing, if not incurable, source of strife. He is undoubtedly a man of talent, information, and experience. He enjoys considerable repute as a member of the Senate of the Empire, and as a business drudge, but his temper is apt to be violent and overbearing, and his prejudices are wholly insurmountable. He told me that he had long ceased to have any correspondence with the United States: but he showed me, hanging up in his apartment, a striking miniature likeness of Mr. Gallatin, which had been executed for him by a lady of Geneva, and a bad oil painting of President Washington, which he had brought with him from America. Washington and Gallatin made to unite in the taste of a Russian "Littérateur et homme d'affaires" as symbols of our republic!

At Count Nesselrode's, last evening, I had a long and somewhat interesting conversation with Baron Brunoff, who holds an important post in the Department of Foreign Affairs. He accompanied the Vice-Chancellor to the coronation of the Austrian Emperor, this summer, at Milan. He invited me to explain the cause of President Jackson's hostility to the Bank, and listened attentively to the detail, expressing a lively astonishment, at its close, that the subject had never before been so clearly and satisfactorily stated. He said that he had heretofore ascribed the controversy to some personal motive of Jackson's; but that he now perceived distinctly that it had its foundation in the settled principles of our Democratic party. Mr. Schwastoff, he said, had informed him that in the United States any corporation or individual might issue paper currency or notes, and that people were *bound by law to accept these in payment of debts!* I explained the temporary effect of a suspension of specie payments, and of the consequent panic, but removed the absurdity of Mr. Schwastoff. He then complained that it proved very difficult to get correct ideas of the state of things in America; that Baron Krudener had certainly formed many false notions from habits of reserve in personal intercourse, and perhaps from his defect in hearing. I pointed out, as the great source of delusion on this side of the Atlantic as to matters in America, the habit of relying upon extracts made by English editors from our commercial newspapers; these newspapers being in trading towns along the sea-coast, dependent upon the patronage and uttering the language of bankers and traders only, while the great voice of the interior and governing people never reached Europe, except in its effects,—that is, in their constant political triumphs. After a very long talk he expressed himself extremely obliged to me for the views I had given. His wife is a lady of Stockholm, of great early beauty. He is himself devoted to business, and has the air, when met in society, of a man perfectly exhausted by his day's drudgery.

1838. *November* 2.—We went late this evening to visit the family of Mr. Bludoff, Minister of the Interior. This gentleman, who I should take to be about sixty, is much esteemed for ability and great devotion to his official duties. He resembles in figure, without being quite as stout or ungraceful, Mr. Woodbury. He has a wife, a son, and a daughter. He has neither nobility nor wealth to recommend him, though probably highly connected. His present residence is a splendid palace in the rear of the Alexandrina Theatre, recently fitted up as the official residence of whoever may fill his post. It is built and furnished in a style suited only to an occupant of an immense fortune, capable and willing to entertain sumptuously. What an inconvenient position to place a man in! He lives and has his chancery on the first floor, his wife on the second floor, and his daughter on the third floor,—each floor being an endless suite of vast and gorgeous apartments, adapted to receive the Imperial court. The mother and daughter are quite attractive persons; neither of them having any personal beauty, but both, the latter particularly, having much intelligence and great amiability.

1838. *November* 4.—Dr. Lefevre being on a visit to us this morning, I took occasion to inquire as to the received opinions here on the subject of the Homœopathic system of medicine. He spoke of it with great candour, and with obvious knowledge on the subject. He said that some time ago the hope of saving about three millions of roubles per annum in drugs, etc., induced the government to try the system in some of the military hospitals; it there failed entirely, the patients died in countless numbers. The small doses are totally inefficacious where the disorder is fixed and serious. In ordinary practice complaints are light, nervous, and transient, and the homœopath may therefore often seem to produce effects which time and a little care would accomplish. He is inflexible in exacting, as a part of his prescription, scrupulous attention to diet, exercise, clothing, early sleep, etc., and these achieve infinitely more than his medicines. To a certain extent, therefore, the system is useful. But Lefevre suggests that the homœopath does what the regular physician never does, and what therefore leaves the practice open to suspicion and doubt,—he is his own apothecary or compounder, and takes from his pocket what he directs to be swallowed. No one, therefore, knows exactly what or how much he administers. He writes out no prescription and is unchecked by a scientific druggist; nevertheless the doctor thinks that the system enjoys favour here, and is probably advancing in estimation.

Count Rossi, who arrived here about two weeks since as Minister from the King of Sardinia, and who visited us this evening, is a remarkably handsome man, apparently nearly forty years of age. Six feet high, with a figure like that of Christopher Hughes, though more erect and compact, and with blue eyes, light hair, and soft, florid complexion; his manners are well formed and polished, and he produces an agreeable impression; he speaks English, though indifferently. He spoke of knowing Mr. Davezac, our Minister formerly at the Hague (at present, I believe, also), and has certainly a just conception of his character. He had also well known Mr. and Mrs. Browne while they were in Paris, and upon being told their unhappy fate, manifested feeling and respect.

1838. *November* 5.—The *presentation* at the British Ambassador's was attended this evening. We went at half-past eight o'clock *en grande tenue*, as the etiquette of the occasion demanded. I am told that this ceremonial, as a means of introducing the highest grade of diplomatic functionaries to their colleagues and to the fashionable world, is peculiar to this Court. Marquis of Clanricarde is a tall, thin man, somewhat bald, with a fine eye and prepossessing manner; his features are awkwardly set together, and produce an unfavourable impression at first. Lady Clanricarde, the daughter of Canning, and the mother of seven children, is thoroughly English in figure, style, expression, and speech; her features are prominent, and indicate intelligence as well as past beauty. He is about thirty-nine and she about thirty-five years of age. He looks perhaps younger than he is; she, on the contrary, seems older than she is. Their reception of our party was certainly kind. The whole of Butera's second floor was thrown open, and the stairway thronged with Russians dressed in splendid English liveries. The visitors were not as numerous as I expected to find them;

but probably a number have reserved themselves for tomorrow night, which is embraced by the invitation. I recognized Mr. Buchanan, who is secretary or attaché to the Embassy, as having been in America with Sir Charles Vaughan. He told me that Sir Charles had been appointed Ambassador to Constantinople, but owing to some sudden cause had never gone there; that he had, however, obtained the rank, and was now content to retire upon the pension incident to it.

1838. *November 7.*—The career of entertainments began to-day by a dinner of the French Ambassador; Mrs. Dallas and myself present. There were forty-eight at table, among whom were Count and Countess Nesselrode; Count and Countess Woronzow, Count Charnicheff, Prince Volkonsky, the Marquis and Marchioness of Clanricarde, with all the rest of the diplomatic leading missions, Princess Beloselsky, Princess Soltikoff, etc. Prince Kosloffsky, who came in after dinner, informed Mrs. Dallas that the Empress had appeared at the great theatre last night, and had introduced her daughter the Grand Duchess Marie (I presume by the peculiar style of her dress) to the public as about becoming a bride.

1838. *November 9.*—Mrs. Daschkoff visited Mrs. Dallas to-day, full of the gossip of the town. The Russians dislike the British Ambassador and Ambassadress. Their presentation of Tuesday evening last was attended by very few, and her Ladyship has been exceedingly indignant. Her manner is represented as excessively haughty and cold, as indicating an extravagant self-esteem. She dressed, too, in full black, which Russians construe as opposite to the joy and pride with which she ought in her appearance to welcome her visitors.

Her husband, too, has shocked the nerves of the moral fashionables of this Court by the arrival of his mistress on the last steamer; he thinks, too, of nothing but hunts and races, and wants the dignity of an Ambassador.

1838. *November* 13.—The water of the Neva rose during the night under the influence of a strong southwesterly wind, and at ten o'clock this morning was swollen five feet above its customary level. It appeared in the streets, through the gratings of the common sewers. Having advanced just far enough to awaken anxiety, it suddenly receded and fell.

A combination of incidents and reflections strongly impels me to the belief that a war between England and Russia is on the eve of explosion. The movements in India indicate an apprehension that the Russian forces are uniting with those at Persia to assist the native princes to change their masters. Russia is perceptibly mortified, if not angered, by the ascendency which England has recently exercised over the counsels of the Turkish Sultan and of the Austrian Emperor. England is exasperated by the results of the blockade of the coast of Circassia; by the progress of Don Carlos in Spain, traceable almost exclusively to the aid, moral and material, of Russia; and by the gradual but certain development of Russian manufactures. The Ministry, too, must make some appeal to the loyalty and prejudices of the country, or they are gone. In the late *Globe*, the Emperor has been personally and most violently assailed, and this is the special paper of Lord Palmerston; and I cannot avoid observing that the new British Ambassador, Marquis Clanricarde, has been received with coldness, if not neglect. There is also existing among the lower classes, the merchants, officers of the army, etc., a feverish sense of impending conflict. Suppose this war to come, what may be its effects upon the United States? Its effects upon our commerce with this empire would seem to be obvious and immediate. It must wholly cease. There are few Russian ports, and their natural difficulty of access would be made insurmountable by the vexations of British blockades. The trade, too, which cannot be carried on here will probably be drawn by England towards herself; we shall sell her the cotton, tobacco, and sugar which would otherwise be brought here to be exchanged for Russian products. Politically we might soon be drawn into the conflict; Russia would re-excite the Canadians; impressment would come again into practice; it would be seen that we could avail ourselves of the opportunity to dispose of the northeast boundary question, the northwest boundary, etc.

1838. *November* 15.—The first *soirée* of the season at Count Woronzow's was numerously and brilliantly attended; Mrs. Dallas accompanied me. The British Ambassadors and Ambassadresses with their respective suites, the rest of the diplomatic corps, Monseigneur the Grand Duke Michel, Count and Countess Strogonoff, recently Ambassadorial representatives from this Court at the Coronation of Queen Victoria, etc., were present. General Tschitchérine intimated that the Marquis of Clanricarde was not held in high estimation here, that his private character was believed to be bad, and it was said that he had been separated from his wife for some time. I was congratulated on the news from the United States by Mr. Buchanan. The messenger of Galignani and a letter received from Mr. Benjamin Rush contain intelligence of the successful result in the elections of Pennsylvania, New Jersey, Maryland, and probably Georgia. These States, added to those already certain—Maine, New Hampshire, South Carolina, Alabama, Missouri, Illinois, Michigan, and Arkansas—constitute a squadron which leaves no room for future apprehension as to the national administration. I trust David R. Porter's majority is sufficiently decisive. My prediction has always been that it would exceed twenty thousand. I took care by a conversation with Count Brunoff that Count Nesselrode should hear my views of the conclusive character of these elections, as I have sometimes thought that an impression prevailed here that our Democratic ascendency was on the eve of extinction. I beat Count Litta a capital game of chess.

1838. *November* 16.—It snowed considerably this evening and the frost seems steadily advancing. We went to the *soirée* of Princess Razoumoffsky. It was but partially attended. She is a lady of about sixty, of unincumbered personal position, of apparently great stability of health, and of about five hundred thousand roubles " de rentes." Her parties are regularly given every Friday throughout the year, in town or in the country. Her rooms, about ten in succession, are not large; but they are ornamented with a luxury and profuse expenditure not to be surpassed. The folding-doors opening into her " cabinet," chambre à coucher, " à bain," are rich beyond conception, and attracted universal attention; their substance seemed to be a sort of rose amber, richly inlaid. I beat Mr. Tschitchérine at chess.

No book could have given me more amusement than I have derived during the last week from Chateaubriand's " Congress of Verona." It is in two good-sized octavos. The objects of the author would seem to be a vindication of his statesmanship while Minister in the department of Foreign Affairs in 1822–'23–'24, a period of about sixteen months, under Louis the XVIII.; a claim to the exclusive merit of the war waged successfully by France against Spain for the deliverance of King Ferdinand from the power of the Cortes; and a development of the views and operations of the author in reference to the question of the independence of the American Spanish colonies; an exhibition of the manner in which he was dismissed and a denial of his having intrigued for the place of Count Villèle, then at the head of the Ministry. The manner in which this most eloquent writer pursues these purposes is extremely attractive. To be sure, he manifests all the conceited egotism and much of the deceitfulness of the French politician; but his fancy is so rich, his political imagery and diction are so glowing and soft, his recurrence to classical reminiscences are so frequent and agreeable, the original letters and documents which he publishes, interspersed in his narrative, are so interesting, and his delineations of the most remarkable personages of his official time are so vivid and true, that I think he has produced two volumes which surpass Wraxall or Cumberland. The Congress of Verona was one of those regular royal conspiracies against constitutional forms of government and popular rights of which we have seen many, and are destined to see more before the struggles of the two principles can possible cease. At it were convened not merely great sovereigns, one of whom, Alexander of Russia, was really great, but there were also Wellington, Metternich, Nesselrode, and Chateaubriand,— names destined to long fame. It is striking, if not alarming, to find this Congress entertained, even for a moment, the idea of planting in Mexico and Colombia a race of Bourbon monarchs. We had a more direct interest in these princely combinations than we imagined. The rapid sketch of the life and character of the autocrat is very fine; the pervading hostility towards the Austrian statesman is a redeeming feature; and the letters of Cobbett and Canning are as characteristic and admirable as possible. There is, on the whole, to be sure, a most appalling picture of heartless political cunning and duplicity, but ill assorted with the conscious immortality and daring independence of the author of "La Génie du Christianisme."

1838. *November* 18.—Baron Manderstrom, Baron Schleinitz, Marquis Carréga, Mr. Buchanan, and Mr. Chew dined with me to-day, and remained unusually long. It would seem to be understood that the Emperor of Russia will quit this for Moscow on Wednesday next with the Duke de Leuchtenberg; that the marriage of the Grand Duchess Marie will not take place before the first week in July next, and that the sovereigns of Austria and Prussia will attend it. Mr. Buchanan condemned the resignation of Lord Durham with great warmth, and was convinced that on his arrival in England he would be denounced by all parties.

1838. *November* 22.—Mr. S. Cramer, whom I visited this evening, informed me that a most remarkable incident in the trade from St. Petersburg had occurred this fall, of which he knew no example during his forty years' activity as a merchant. All the hemp brought for export had been purchased and shipped to England at nearly twice the ordinary price; and all the tallow. The orders had been thus numerous and extravagant owing to the prevailing opinion in England that a war would break out with this country. There is in mercantile sagacity, the keenness of self-interest, something that foretells the future as surely as anything else.

An event of a singular character has set us all speculating. The Emperor in a single-horse sledge, without any attendant, was seen to stop at the British Embassy and to go in. He stayed for half an hour. Was this a visit to the Ambassador or to his lady? What does it mean? Is it in order to crush at once the rumour of an impending war? or is it the last civility preparatory to hostilities? One is apt to scan closely the most trifling actions of so eminent a personage, especially in connection with public characters. And yet his Majesty is really so fond of personal eccentricity of movement, liking to surprise and to go where least expected, that nothing can be safely deduced from his individual acts. He has started this evening, though it snows rapidly, for Moscow, accompanied by his intended son-in-law, the Duke of Leuchtenberg, planning to be two days in going, four days in remaining, and two days in returning.

1838. *November* 26.—The ball of Madame Boutourlin. We went at near eleven o'clock and returned at half-past three. The Grand Duke Michel was there, and all the diplomatic corps. Boutourlin, who prides himself upon his collection, and who, by the by, is the author of the "Russian Campaign to Paris," has got, within the last few months, from Rome a beautiful piece of sculpture by Bartolini; it is a female slave seated upon her lower legs, in a position scarcely practicable by even Taglioni, with her hands joined near her knees, and her head thrown a little upwards and backwards. The figure is perfectly naked, perhaps rather too thin, but on the whole graceful, soft, and effective. The richness of choice Parian marble, when fresh, can scarcely be imagined by those who have not seen it.

1838. *December* 1.—Dined at five P.M. with the Minister from Denmark, Baron Blome. He is an old bachelor seventy years of age; Danish in every part of his appearance; prominent features, large mouth, florid complexion, weak eyes, red and powdered hair; mild and agreeable in his manners and conversation; very rich and hospitable. His eyes are so bad he cannot go out at night, and in his own house every light is carefully shaded. He has resided at this port for forty years. Is the indefatigable attendant at all military reviews, wearing scarlet and white with countless crosses and stars, and is almost a universal favourite. The French and British Ambassadors were the chief guests, Count Nesselrode being unwell and absent. A number of Russians were at table, among them Count Litta, Count Borsh, Zavadowsky, Obriscoff, Prince Kosloffsky.

1838. *December* 4.—Mr. Soltikoff, while spending this evening with us, narrated several anecdotes with great spirit, which it may be worth while to preserve. He is a man about sixty-five years of age, of immense wealth, and of great talent, it is said. He was formerly high in Imperial favour, but, owing to some personal indiscretion in his manners at court, he was obliged to retire, at least from intimacy. It is a fact remarkably illustrative of the little attention which the United States receive from European savans, that Mr. Soltikoff, although unquestionably eminent for ability and erudition, and though he has a copy of the Declaration of Independence, with autograph signatures, hanging up in his library, did not know that General Washington had ever been President, but

thought that he had retired wholly from public affairs,
from the peace of 1783 to the period of his death! He
would hardly believe me when I assured him that he had
been our chief magistrate for eight years under the existing Constitution. Mr. Soltikoff says that the inundation of the Neva in 1824 was very sudden and incon-
ceivably disastrous in its effects. He occupied the house
in which he now lives in the Small Moscoy, and was
sitting at his office-table sealing some letters and pack-
ages. He had felt an unusual coldness in his feet; he
rang the bell for his servant, and ordered him to take
some letters to the post-office, and to his utter amazement he received for answer that it was impossible, as
the waters were six feet high in the streets and still
rushing upwards. He had scarcely been told this before
the floor on which he stood burst and opened and the
waters rose in his apartment up to his own middle; he
scrambled up-stairs, directing that nothing should be
removed; this swell lasted for about six hours. The
Emperor Alexander was born in 1777, a year memorable
by a similar inundation, and when that of 1824 occurred,
he said it announced his approaching end, and became
an altered man. Soltikoff describes the change as
striking and distressing; the calamity seemed to be
forever present in all its horror to his mind, and to
weigh him down. One melancholy incident he particularly dwelt upon, that of an old woman whom he saw
while he was wandering about to relieve the sufferers,
and who was eagerly searching for the corpse of a young
and only grandson. The Emperor offered her ten thousand roubles, which she declined receiving, saying she
wanted nothing but the body, and continued to weep
and search, when suddenly she espied the object of her

pursuit covered with dirt and rubbish, and rushed to it frantic with delight, and embraced and clung to it in prolonged delirium.

When, in the campaign of 1814, the allies entered Paris, the Emperor Alexander separated himself from his staff, and, in the confidence of good intentions towards the French people, confidently rode alone and in advance. He was stopped by a knot of *poissardes*, one of whom advanced and presented him a handsome bouquet of flowers, saying that he was the only one of the monarchs whom they loved.

During his stay at Paris, Alexander was in the habit of almost daily visiting the Empress Josephine at Malmaison; and, indeed, it was owing to his energetic friendship at the Congress of Vienna that Eugene Beauharnais, Duke of Leuchtenberg, was allowed to retain Bavaria. On one occasion, driving out to see the ex-Empress in his carriage, with four horses abreast, and galloping, as usual, he met a French officer in a rich curricle and pair. The Frenchman would not yield the road, but cried out, "Give way! give way!" and the consequence was that when the two equipages encountered the curricle was overturned and broken to pieces, its horses knocked down and much wounded, and their owner thrown out, rendered perfectly furious with rage. The Emperor alighted immediately, begged the officer's pardon, hoped he was not hurt, and ascribed the disaster to the carelessness of his coachman. "No!" was the reply. "You are doubtless one of those who have conquered our capital, and you think to ride rough-shod over us; but I will not submit to such indignities and wrongs. I demand the satisfaction due to an insulted man. There is my address, and I expect to see you by eleven o'clock to-morrow morning." "Agreed," said his Majesty; "you shall be satisfied." Early the next day the Emperor sent General Kissilieff to the Frenchman with a splendid curricle and two of his finest horses, requesting him to accept them in lieu of the injured ones. At first the Frenchman haughtily declined, saying that he waited the personal presence of General Kissilieff's friend and associate, and would receive nothing but the satisfaction of an apology or a duel. He was thunderstruck, says Mr. Soltikoff, and overwhelmed, when Kissilieff replied, "That is impossible. My friend is his Majesty the Emperor of Russia."

1838. *December* 6.—This, according to the Greek calendar, is St. Catherine's Day, and therefore the "Name's Day" of all ladies Catherine. Much is made of the Name's Day, and complimentary visits of felicitation are all the go. The name of Catherine is a favourite one in the fashionable circle. We manifested our attention to the custom by going at nine in the evening to Princess Hohenlohe's. We met there Madame Youskoff, the mother of the Princess, Princess Sophia Modene, her sister, Madame Paschkoff, Marquis De Villafranca, Marquis De Carréga, and a few others. Hohenlohe showed me his whole house, into which he has just removed; it is the property of his wife.

I do not recollect to have seen the following anecdote, which is given me as illustrative of the political finesse of the Empress, Catherine II., but which is probably an invention. Charles J. Fox had for some time been very hostile to Russia and its sovereign in the House of Commons. The Empress gave a large entertainment at the Hermitage, to which she invited several distinguished Englishmen who happened to be here at the time. In one of the rooms there was a plaster cast of Fox, which was surrounded by busts of Cicero, Demosthenes, etc., and in this apartment, and near the busts, the Empress had engaged herself at whist. In the course of the evening her English guests sauntered into her neighbourhood, and, seeing the cast, expressed aloud to each other their surprise. The Empress frowned, listened for a moment, and then said to them, " What! gentlemen, are you surprised to see that bust in the midst of the greatest orators? Do you think me incapable of doing justice to an enemy? I can give Mr. Fox the rank to which his wonderful ability entitles him, even while I suffer under its exertions." These words were carefully reported to Fox, who soon afterwards became the Parliamentary friend and eulogist of Catherine. The plaster cast soon gave way to one of marble and another of bronze.

1838. *December* 8.—The celebrated Court choir was visited to-day during one of its public rehearsals. This musical band—altogether vocal—is especially assigned to the Imperial chapel. It is said to consist of about one hundred and fifty voices, though we certainly had not more than sixty this morning, of whom twenty were boys between the ages of ten and thirteen. These choristers are selected with great care in every part of the empire, by virtue of a standing order which directs that the discovery of a remarkably fine voice in child or adult shall be immediately followed by his being forwarded to St. Petersburg. They are taught and exercised with great care; they are said to make the finest sacred harmony witnessed in Europe. It is so perfect as to resemble a rich and magnificent organ. I could scarcely, at first, believe that what I heard was the human voice alone. The effect produced upon those who are peculiarly sensitive to music is overpowering; some have wept, others fainted. The two Embassies and Countess Strogonoff were there, but the audience was mixed and did not exceed four hundred.

1838. *December* 13.—At half-past ten went to a ball at Count Levaschoff's. It was exceedingly brilliant. Prince Hohenlohe apprised me that the diplomatic body would be invited to attend the ceremony of affiancing the Grand Duchess Marie and the Duke De Leuchtenberg on Sunday next, with their respective ladies. This necessarily involves a special and unexpected expenditure of at least two hundred and fifty dollars, which I can no more avoid than I could avoid returning the Emperor's salute as I pass him in the street, and yet I am expected to meet all such charges out of my salary!

I met at Count Levaschoff's Count Frederick Pahlen, formerly Minister in the United States. He has been here for two weeks only, usually residing in the country, and I heard by mere accident of his being in the room. He saluted me with great cordiality, remembered the hospitality of my father, and inquired about many whom he knew in the United States. I cannot say that I should have ever recognized him. His manner is ardent, his hair light, his eyes blue, his complexion florid, his figure an easy and gentlemanly one, indicating a man turned of fifty, and he spoke English fluently. He has two brothers in Paris, one of whom had been with him in America.

1838. *December* 14.—A printed programme of the ceremonies to be observed on the betrothment of the Grand Duchess Marie was sent to me by the Grand Master of Ceremonies early this morning. This subject is now the absorbing one. The programme as a means of precise and practical information is defective in several particulars; it does not expressly mention the Ambassadors; it does not specially provide for the disposition of the wives of the Foreign Ministers; and it leaves an impression that the secretaries and attachés are to be excluded in the parade. In the course of the day we have also received two invitations, one addressed to myself, in language that would seem to embrace the secretary of legation, and the other addressed to Mrs. Dallas.

During the long and interesting *tête-à-tête* with General Tschitchérine, several characteristic anecdotes of Lord Durham were told. Tschitchérine was his personal friend, and on all occasions of excitement his confidential adviser. Durham he describes as a man of fine abilities and *au fond* of excellent intentions, but subject to violent excesses of passion and of inordinate vanity. He set out with the determination to make himself individually acceptable to the Emperor, who had delighted him by his manners on visiting the frigate on which he arrived in Cronstadt. When the recovery of the Emperor from the accident of overturning his carriage, by which his arm was broken, was announced, Durham resolved, if possible, to make his personal congratulations. He called on Tschitchérine, and, disclaiming all diplomatic motive or purpose, asked how he could accomplish his desire. The General proposed his going with him at once to Peterhoff, and there ascertaining what could be done. They started immediately, and on their arrival waited upon Prince Volkonsky, who was at first entirely at a loss how to act. Durham suggested the expedience of his passing off as a sort of messenger sent for inquiry by the Chasseur of the British Ambassador, as a mode which would get rid of forms. The plan was frankly stated to the Emperor, who laughed at its ingenuity, and kept him for several days at the palace.

Lady Mary Lambson, the daughter of Durham, rode out on horseback accompanied only by her brother-in-law. On passing through one of the gates of the city, the sentinel, as usual, and as ordered, not knowing them, offered to stop them merely to ascertain their object. This is always done as a mere matter of course. Lady Mary, however, probably unable to understand or be understood, rode on without satisfying the soldier, who immediately dropped the huge bar to arrest her progress; the bar fell on the rear of the horse, fortunately missing herself, but frightening and startling the animal. When this was reported to Durham, he became furious, flew to Tschitchérine, and, throwing himself into an arm-chair, gave vent to an ungovernable fit of passion, beginning with the exclamation, "What do you think? One of your vagabond soldiery has been on the eve of killing my daughter!" Much time and persuasion were necessary before he could be calmed, and he dwelt with prolonged exasperation upon the fact that the sentinel had smiled or grinned when he saw the horse of Lady Mary Lambson start. Finally, it was agreed that he should make no mention of the subject at all, except to the Emperor in person, and then very briefly, and only in the manner of narrative without complaint. Durham, however, forgot himself the very next day, and, being at a large dinner alongside of Count Nesselrode, turned round, and with a loud, excited voice repeated all the circumstances of the affair. The Vice-Chancellor strove to stop his vehemence by calmly remarking that the topic was not one for a large and mixed company, at least to be addressed to him. This only poured oil upon the fire of the enraged father, and he poured forth a torrent of invective, dropping in his heat the term "barbarian." The attention of the whole table had been drawn; the Russians were extremely offended with the manner and epithets of the Ambassador; his words were exaggerated and circulated everywhere; the whole society of St. Petersburg were on the point of apprising his Lordship that he had gone too far, when General Tschitchérine stepped in, visited in every direction with explanatory and soothing remarks, and finally prevailed in tranquillizing the storm.

In the course of the evening, Mr. Kaiserveldt made himself very entertaining by a number of anecdotes of his own personal experience. His description of the scene which took place at the Imperial chapel when the young Grand Duke became of age, and took the oath of allegiance, gave a delightful impression of the domestic feelings of the autocrat and his family. He says that the church was thronged with the high prelates of the church and dignitaries of state; a small table was placed in the centre, on which were placed the Bible, some religious emblems, and the written draft of the oath to be taken; after some prefatory ceremonies the Emperor led his son to the desk, pointed to the scroll, and bade him read attentively and aloud the oath before he signed it. The young man began audibly and distinctly; but when he came to that part which imported that he vowed obedience and love to the Emperor his father, his voice faltered, choked, and finally ceased; he seemed to be overpowered by his feelings, and wept profusely. The Emperor, who stood close by, remained motionless and gave no symptom of agitation except two heavy tears that rolled down his cheeks; a second time did the son endeavour to proceed, but again failed under the tenderest emotions about his father. The Czar allowed some minutes to elapse that he might master himself, and then with all the apparent unmoved dignity of the monarch pointed again to the scroll. As soon as he had completed the oath, the Grand Duke threw himself into his father's arms, where he sobbed aloud for an instant, when, recollecting his mother to be at the side of the church, he rushed towards her and was received with an affecting and prolonged embrace. The Emperor, unable farther to control himself, went to them while thus clinging to each other, and encircling them both with his arms gave way to a paroxysm of emotion. In this scene, says Mr. Kaiserveldt, there was no acting; it was a sudden and obviously wholly unexpected overflow of parental and filial love; it drew tears from all who beheld it.

A little of the personal history of Count Levaschoff justifies the highest opinion I had contracted of him from his manners and conversation and appearance. He is not what is termed wealthy here; having an income of three hundred thousand roubles, or sixty thousand dollars, only; but he manages what he has with an economy and care which enable him to live in the utmost splendour and with unbounded hospitality. His establishment is one of the most attractive in St. Petersburg, and anywhere else would be considered princely in its extent; his drawing-rooms are flanked by beautiful gardens and by an immense green-house crowded even at this season with luxuriant flowers and tropical fruits, hung with birds, and lighted up for promenades, etc., accessible to his guests by wide stone stairways, and at the extremity of this range is a *ménage* where he keeps enough to accommodate a regiment. He is now, and has long been, a great favourite among the highest nobility, and proved his title to their esteem not long ago by the manner in which he conducted a quarrel with his sovereign himself. At that time he had been governor of a province for some years, and unfortunately had a dispute with the celebrated Marshal Sacken, using language on one occasion of considerable severity, but just. Sacken addressed the Emperor, saying that he was now too old to publish insults offered to him, but that he devolved his honour to the care and vindication of his master. Levaschoff was called to the capital; he adhered to the propriety of his course, and was dismissed from his office. He retired to the rendezvous of all discontented nobles, Moscow, and seemed resolved not to return to St. Petersburg. The Emperor perceived public sentiment to be entirely with the Count, and frankly and more fully reconsidered the whole subject. In a short time a post of greater dignity and importance than the one he had occupied was assigned to him. His friends wished him to decline it. "No," said Levaschoff; "I will act as the Emperor has a right to expect, as one sensible of the extent of the *amende honorable* thus offered, and I will finally do what is due to my own honour." He went to the department allotted to him, then in great disorder; he put its affairs in admirable condition, reported in full upon every branch of its business and interest, and when the Emperor expressed his gratification he immediately resigned. Since then he has lived wholly in this city, has by slow degrees become perfectly reconciled, and enjoys at present the favour of his sovereign and the respect of all who know him.

1838. *December* 15.—It is now ascertained that the diplomatic corps, including the secretaries, are all invited to the ceremony of to-morrow, although the heads of the missions only will find places in the chapel.

1838. *December* 16.—At eleven o'clock this morning I went, accompanied by Mrs. Dallas and Mr. Chew, all *en grande tenue*, to the Imperial palace of the Hermitage. The accumulation of equipages on the river front probably induced our being invited to alight and enter at the door in the Milione, as we were driving on. The British Ambassador and Ambassadress had just preceded us. We passed through several rooms until we came to the one temporarily converted into a chapel, and crossing that we were ushered through two serried lines of brilliantly-equipped officers along the Vatican gallery or corridor, and into the apartment appropriated to the reception of the diplomatic corps. We were early, none of our colleagues but Clanricarde and his suite being there, and the customary guard of grenadiers not stationed until ten or fifteen minutes afterwards. Lady Clanricarde was handsomely and tastefully dressed in a silk of deep blue, fronted with a costly show of point lace, and having an extensive train bordered with the same and richly worked with Roman pearls; her head glittered with a coronet of diamonds, whose lustre, however, seemed to fade when contrasted with those of the Russian Court. Our associates soon arrived. The Ambassadress of France wore a gorgeous but obviously old dress, white with a profusion of gold tinsel, and a train of crimson velvet embroidered in gold. Countess Schimmelpenninck was overwhelmed with finery of all sorts and of all colours; silver and gold tinsel, jewels of every description, a train fringed with silver, an upper gown of gauze fretted with silver stars, and a half turban. Contrasted with these, the white satin gown, with light-pink satin train flounced with tulle, and a head-dress of a few flowers (the costume of Mrs. Dallas) unadorned by a single jewel of any sort, struck me as exceedingly modest, peculiarly suited to an American lady, and, withal, really much the prettiest. The English and Austrian Ambassadors wore their military uniforms of scarlet and white, only differing in the collocation of the colours,—the first having scarlet coat and white pantaloons, the latter having white coat and scarlet pantaloons. Baron Barante was in civil dress, richly covered with embroidery. Baron Blome, the Dane, resembled the Englishman, except that he glittered with more crosses and ribbons. Count Rossi, the Sardinian (whose wife is not yet out of her room), wore a remarkably becoming military dress of green and gold, turned up with white. Count d'Appony, the Austrian attaché, exhibited his fanciful and favourite costume of the Hungarian nobleman and ranger. The ceremonies began by the Ambassadors and Ministers (without their ladies or secretaries) being conducted, in due order of rank, to the large and lofty square apartment arranged into a chapel, and stationed along one side of it, with their chief, Count Ficquelmont, nearest the door at which it was known the Imperial family would enter. A screen of the necessary size, with its external panels beautifully painted with saints and Scriptural subjects, its parts movable on hinges, and having two doors in front, was fixed on the eastern side of the room, and formed the retiring and preparing recess of the priests. Between its two doors was the altar, and on both sides of this screen, within a small low railing, were the Court choir. Directly in the centre, and at a short distance from the screen, was a platform about ten feet square, raised, say a foot or more, from the floor, and covered with crimson velvet bordered with gold lace. A small table was on this platform, and the rest of the apartment was divested of furniture in order to make room. The large glass chandelier in the middle was illuminated, and when we entered there were assembled only a few of the highest civil and military officers. About thirty of the clergy officiated, three of whom were of the highest rank, and one of these the very old, gray-haired, and enfeebled Metropolitan; three others were of a secondary rank; the bonnets or mitres of these six were worn during most of the ceremony, and were ornamented with miniatures, pearls, and other jewels in great abundance. The robes of all who officiated were of a material which resembled rich, thick, cut velvet of a glowing crimson colour, with golden crosses worked in it in every direction, and with broad stripes of gold embroidery sunk, as it were, in the velvet. The manner in which these robes are adjusted is rather clumsy; they seem to be thrown over the shoulders, as one would throw a sheet or table-cloth, when intending that it should conceal the whole figure, without regard to grace or fitness. We had not been long in this apartment when we heard the customary suppressed " *hush*" which, on such occasions, precedes the Imperial family, and we, of course, fell into our line. The "*Fourriers* Chambellans," etc., in double-file and in their richest liveries, passed in at the northern door and went out at the southern one. The Grand Master of Ceremonies and the Grand Marshal of the Court, with two or three other high dignities, bearing large golden square staves surmounted with crowns of brilliants or gold work, quitted the lengthened procession, and stationed themselves at the extremity of the diplomatic line and in front of the velveted platform. Then entered the Emperor, Empress, their second son, Constatine, their two other sons, the Grand Duke Michel, and his Grand Duchess Helen, the Grand Duchesses Marie, Olga, and Alexandra, and the betrothed (or "promis"), the Duke of Leuchtenberg. At the threshold the Imperial party were met by the whole of the clergy, the Metropolitan at their head, bearing a sumptuous silver cross, with a golden full-length image of the crucified Saviour upon it, and another carrying the chalice of holy water, drops of which were scattered by a sort of short bouquet of green leaves. Each of the Imperial family kissed the cross, held up for that purpose by the Metropolitan, and his hand also; and each, bowing forward as if to approach the chalice of holy water, received a few drops, from the bouquet, on the palm of the hand, which they carried to their lips. They then crossed the room and ranged themselves immediately opposite to us, the Emperor leaning his back against the edge of the open door, through which could be seen an endless vista of magnificently-dressed ladies, unable to get accommodations in the chapel. Directly behind the Imperial family, I was unexpectedly pleased to find that the ladies of the foreign Ministers followed. My friend Count Schimmelpenninck had not noticed this; and when the throng of maids of honour had passed by, and had (as many as could) arranged themselves throughout the room, he abruptly turned to me and said, " I believe I will go home." " What for, Count?" " This neglect of our ladies is not to be borne; you perceive they have been left with the secretaries and attachés in that remote antechamber." Had such been the fact, and

AT THE COURT OF THE CZAR. 145

had I, as probably I should have, encouraged the Count by the slightest assenting movement, we must have had an agreeable little flare-up. As it was, I relieved my colleague by pointing out to him his own wife, safely ensconced by my own, close to the Imperial family. The betrothment began by his Majesty's conducting his daughter Marie and the Duke to the platform, the latter being placed on the right of the former, and the Emperor returning to his former position. A lighted wax taper was then placed by two of the priests in the hands of each of the affianced. Religious exercises followed in the Greek form, of which I could understand nothing. Two priests brought on large golden plates the wedding-rings, and deposited them on the small tables, that of the Grand Duchess, which I could distinctly scan, was a very large diamond of extreme brilliancy. The Metropolitan, with some ceremony, placed each ring on the finger of its owner; and after other recitations the Empress went forward, took the ring off the hand of Marie and placed it on that of the Duke, and the ring off the hand of the Duke and placed it on that of Marie. At this instant, as if the artillery had actually witnessed the movement, a roar of guns issued from the fortress on the opposite side of the Neva, exceeding in number one hundred. The venerable Metropolitan administered to each of the parties the promise or engagement, reading it from one of their sacred volumes, and they, in turn, manifested their assent by kissing the golden cross he held up. They then descended from the platform. The Grand Duchess threw herself into her father's arms, and remained some seconds, clinging to him under the influence of strong emotions; they were embraced by all the Imperial circle in succession, and here seemed to terminate the special act of affiancing. The priests, however, proceeded with their performances, during a short part of which it was very inconveniently necessary for all who were present to kneel. The hymn for the safety of the Emperor, in which the choir joined with great effect, was delightfully executed. When the whole closed, the Imperial family passed out at the door through which they entered, bowing to us as they passed, and were followed by the almost endless train of maids of honour, chamberlains, etc. The ladies of the foreign Ministers went in the current and in the order they came, while the Ministers themselves were detained in the chapel for some time, preparatory to their being led, in the direction opposite to that taken by the Court, the whole way round through the interminable saloons of the palace, until they came to a large and richly-ornamented one overlooking the river, where they again marshalled themselves in line awaiting the coming of the affianced couple, to whom they in due solemnity tendered their felicitations. Here we had been joined by the secretaries and attachés; our ladies being left in the apartment in which they were originally placed, to receive, first, the visit of the Duke and his future Duchess. This ceremony gave me the first opportunity I have had to form any sort of opinion of the young man so suddenly exalted by the Emperor by incorporation into his domestic circle, and into the highest grades of his honours and service. His appearance is prepossessing, though certainly not handsome or striking; his manner is polished and unaffected; he looks about twenty-one years of age, and is about five feet eight inches high, with black hair closely cut, arched black eyebrows, small black moustache, and a lively and expressive black eye. His complexion is rather fair. His nose is like my own—a mean feature—and he has, when smiling, a habit of drawing up his upper lip too far, so that his teeth (not regular nor perfectly white) and his gums are unpleasantly developed. He left us with exceeding grace and self-possession. We now retraced our steps back to our wives, and hurried to our respective homes.

We were urged to attend the Great Theatre to-night, as the Court would be there in gala dress, in honour of the day, and to witness the new ballet by Taglioni, but declined on the single ground of its being our Sabbath. Some of the illuminations of the city, which my children and Mrs. Dallas rode out to see, were uncommonly splendid.

1838. *December* 17.—Mrs. Dallas went with me, at half-past ten, to the French Ambassador's. There were few there. We met Clanricarde coming away as we went in, Count Ficquelmont, Prince Hohenlohe, Baron Seebach, Countess Kreptovitch, Princess Gallitzin, Countess Strogonoff, etc. I got into a long conversation with Barante, parts of which I desire to remember. I began by asking whether there were any modern authors in France, whom he could recommend to me, on the elementary principles of their law, like Blackstone in England, or Kent in the United States? He said there was none: none but those who wrote merely on practice; that their code had, as yet, no enlarged commentators. I told him I had the code, accompanied by the discourses of those who prepared its various branches, and which I esteemed invaluable: but that I had presumed France had given birth to writers on jurisprudence in general, during the last thirty-five years. He advised me to add to my copy of the code a copy of the discussions before the Council of State, on its provisions, which were conducted in the presence of Napoleon, and which he says were published by Ducros. This work he spoke of as of the highest authenticity and interest. As to the personal agency of Bonaparte, he remembered a striking anecdote which recorded one of his best "*mots*," and which he thinks may be found in the discussions referred to. The question before the Council was as to the adoption of the jury. Napoleon was known to be against it; hence, when the topic came up, most of those present opposed the institution with great ability and address. After a protracted session, Bonaparte suddenly turned to the last speaker with the following question: "Can France dispense with publicity in legislation?" "Certainly not," was unanimously answered. "Then she cannot dispense with her jury, and must have it."

Barante conceives that as yet the trial by jury has rather failed than otherwise in France. He complains that juries are perpetually yielding to feelings of compassion, and do not execute the criminal laws to which their agency is confined. They either acquit, even in cases of obvious and acknowledged guilt, or they resort to the expedient allowed by the code, and declare the crime to have been committed under extenuating circumstances, where, in fact, none existed. The selection of the juries is confined to the electoral class, and they do not exceed two hundred thousand. Notwithstanding this, he did not believe that the French juries were as intelligent as the American. I said, Certainly neither as intelligent nor as honest, if the character he gave of their verdicts were correct; nor would they have ever become so as long as their functions were restricted to penal proceedings. I regarded the institution, especially in connection with civil and municipal justice, as the best practical mode of educating citizens in the knowledge of what was right and proper, both as to themselves and others. "This," he said, "might be, but the process of instruction would be slow in France." "Particularly," I replied, "if you keep your right of suffrage so limited. But might not the evil you complain of arise from the character of your laws? My experience satisfies me that there are two things which practically affect the verdict of juries on criminal trial: if your punishments are too severe, they shock natural feelings, and will be defeated; or, if they be ever so mild, if their infliction be reckless and demoralizing, the same consequence will ensue, for juries are averse to subjecting perhaps a first offender, or a criminal not hardened, to a process of imprisonment and shame by which his vices must be confirmed rather than eradicated." He said their penal code was not sanguinary; and as to penitentiary discipline, the reports of those who had visited the United States for the purpose of examining our system and its operation had not been satisfactory.

Was there any probability that the right of suffrage would be extended in France? Barante hoped not; he thought it already too extensive. A poor man, in France, would not be actually bribed by money, but he would always be in favour of the person who would defray the expense of going to the election and would entertain him while there. Such a voter was not an honest one; and yet his observation led him to be convinced that such would be the result wherever the franchise was extended to the poor. I asked him if the voter, in order to vote, had to leave his family and business, and for how long a time. "Generally," he replied, "he must give himself up to that duty exclusively, and mostly at a considerable distance from his home, for three days." "No wonder, then, that a poor man requires to be compensated or indemnified; you ask him to exercise his right by taking the bread out of his children's mouths, and paying extravagantly for three days of idleness; the defect is not in his inability to withstand the law of necessity, but in your electoral arrangements; give him the opportunity to vote near to his home, and without the loss of more than an hour or two, and he will feel no inducement to sell his independence."

Countess Kreptovitch (the elder), remarking that she remembered the time when, thirty or thirty-five years ago, there were but two "*modistes*" in all St. Petersburg; Barante said that on board of a single steamer from Havre during the last summer there had returned from their annual visit to Paris no less than thirty of these fashionable milliners. Count Ficquelmont observed that thirty years ago there was but one apothecary's shop in the city; and Barante added, but one public library or book-store.

1838. *December* 18.—St. Nicholas's Day, and of course the Emperor's "Name's Day." Agreeably to the invitation of the Grand Master of Ceremonies, I went, accompanied by the Secretary of Legation, to the presentation or reception at the palace of the Hermitage at twelve o'clock. It was in all essential respects like that which I have described under date of the 13th of January, 1838. The throng of maids of honour and of military and civil officers was uncommonly numerous and brilliant.

In the evening, at half-past seven, Mrs. Dallas and my daughters accompanied me to the ball at the same palace. Admiral Heyden, the Russian representative at the battle of Navarino, was there: a plain, stolid-looking Dutchman, now far advanced in years and stationed in a sort of retreat at Reval. The Imperial family were all present and remarkably animated. I overwhelmed Count Litta in a rapid game of chess, and was challenged for a future opportunity by Countess Modené and the French Ambassador. At eleven o'clock we supped in the theatre, arranged to form the finest spectacle of the sort I ever beheld; the whole semi-circle in the rear, at the bottom of the stage, being coloured glass from ceiling to floor, and brilliantly lighted from behind. Exquisite music came from behind the variously-stained glass partitions. The table of the Empress stood in the centre of the parterre, glittering with ornaments of gold; that of the Foreign Ministers stood just beyond, groaning under the weight of the most enormous, massive, and beautiful silver imaginable, the centre-piece being a vase of vast capacity, in which I could easily have deposited two of my children, reposing on the backs of four dogs as large as life, and supported by two human figures at the ends, all of it richly and delicately worked. This load of silver would have found its way to the floor through any ordinary dining-table, and I observed that props had been placed underneath. In harmony and proportion with this were dozens of other decorations. Tables were everywhere spread to accommodate fifty, twenty, or a dozen; and the Emperor stationed himself tranquilly at one of the smallest and most retired, between Madame Paschkoff and Madame Krudener, and with Count Orloff, the Grand Duke Michel, the Duke of Leuchtenberg, General Kissilief, etc. The Ambassadors and Ambassadresses sat at the table of the Empress. Our entertainment of viands and wines was excellent. Dancing was resumed for a short time after supper, and we got home by half-past one o'clock, the company breaking up as soon as their Majesties left.

1838. *December* 19.—Went in the evening to witness the representation of the new grand ballet "Hitana," prepared expressly for Taglioni. The piece is splendidly got up, and consists of a succession of magnificent tableaux, without much interest of plot. "Hitana" in the first scene is a child of seven or eight years of age, who dances exquisitely, and is stolen away by the leader of a band of Bohemian or gypsy strollers. Eight or ten years are supposed to elapse between that and the second act, in which Taglioni appears as Hitana and as the favourite danseuse at a great *fête* or *fair*. She is found in the third at the gypsy encampment close to a water-fall and amid the most picturesque scenery; here her lover joins the band, and the process of his initiation gives occasion for a number of striking tableaux. In the fourth act, she has fled for refuge to her original but unknown home, and she gradually recollects the place and the persons about her. In the fifth act, there is exhibited a rich, bustling, and fantastic masquerade, with every variety of graceful and burlesque dancing. The whole affair is ill suited to the peculiar charm of Taglioni, and seems to lessen her dignity and delicacy. In the scene of the fair she introduced the Cachoucha, and executed it with great effect.

1838. *December* 25.—A *soirée* at home for the special benefit of the children on Christmas night. There were besides a number of ladies and gentlemen, among them the Minister of the Interior, Mr. Bloudoff, who in the course of conversation mentioned that he had to-day heard described to the Emperor by Professor Yacobi, of the University of Delft, a most extraordinary experiment. In the progress of his trials with electro-galvanism the Professor procured two plates of brass, linked them somewhat apart, by a conducting wire. One of the plates was deeply engraved, and had in the centre a human figure cut. Having applied the electro-galvanism for some time, it was discovered, to the amazement of the Professor himself, that the plate which had been left plain had received upon its surface the precise figure and words of the engraved one, except that they were now in bass-relief instead of excavated. The result was incomprehensible and inexplicable, but has since been repeatedly attained by the same Professor. The Emperor, utterly unable to conceive the process, resorted to pleasantry to express his surprise, and exclaimed, " Why, at this rate, Mr. Professor, we shall make children by electro-galvanism."

1838. *December* 27.—A diplomatic *soirée* at Princess Hohenlohe's. The British and French Ambassadors, Lieberman, Schimmelpenninck, Villafranca, etc. A lesson given to the Marchioness Clanricarde in the measure and mazes of the mazourka, for which movement and figure she is wholly unfit.

1838. *December* 28.—Prince Hohenlohe, who says that he was in several of the hardest fights of 1812, and was repeatedly wounded, told me that his age was fifty-one. I had thought him younger than myself. In referring to the cold and impracticable forms of social intercourse, he assured me that such a state of things as existed in this capital was to be found nowhere else in Europe. " I have been at this Court," said he, " for thirteen years; I have married a Russian lady; I have been constantly in society, and I have probably become acquainted with five hundred or six hundred persons; but I do not know one Russian intimately, one whom I can rely upon as a friend." I told him I thought such a condition of things was peculiarly the fate of Americans, as they had no titles, nobility, or European distinction or wealth. He said, "Not so, not so; it is the case with every stranger who enters Russia, let his titles, rank, and riches be what they may. Come to Würtemberg, come into any part of Central Europe, and I will engage that you make intimate friendships by scores."

1838. *December* 30.—Went at half-past ten to Countess Nesselrode's; an unusually large and brilliant company assembled, probably under the expectation of hearing the newly-arrived and celebrated pianist, Madame Pleyel. She executed with great power two long and fine pieces on an admirable instrument of Erard's. The Vice-Chancellor, always somewhat fussy at home, wriggled and bravoed in ecstasies. Prince Volkonsky, a young man, sang two French songs with a rich, round, and cultivated voice, and Mademoiselle Bartinieff indulged us with a performance which very few professed operatic musicians could surpass. Madame Pleyel touched the accompaniment. She is about twenty-nine, somewhat tall, with dark eyes and eyebrows, an intellectual expression, and a good figure. The evening furnished the best music I have heard since I crossed the Atlantic.

1839. *January* 3.—Started at ten A.M. to attend the funeral obsequies of General Narischkin, the father of Countess Woronzow, who died at his government in the interior, of a complaint of the liver, in his fiftieth year, late in October last. Mr. Chew accompanied me, both in full uniform, as etiquette exacts. The ceremony took place at the Church of St. Alexander Nefsky, in the presence of a large concourse of distinguished public officers, military and civil. The routine resembled in most respects the burial of Rodofinikine. The coffin was immensely large, containing the embalmed body and probably one or two more enclosures. It was not opened, and was lowered into a vault opened in the floor of the church. Several distinguished ladies were recognized in the rear of the crowd,—Countess Kreptovitch, Princess Razoumoffsky, Madame Scheveits, Madame Seniavin, etc. They were all in deep black. It is unusual for ladies to be present. Although to me the ceremony appeared a tedious mummery, I cannot help suspecting that it is in many of its parts solemn and touching to those who perfectly understand it. The son of the deceased, Dmitri-Narischkin, and Count Woronzow appeared powerfully impressed, and others were affected. I cannot, however, get over the ludicrous form of furnishing the deceased with a passport and a large basin of rice-pudding; these are really too absurd for any age, let alone the nineteenth century. We were detained here until one o'clock.

1839. *January* 10.—Agreeably to former invitation, I went at twelve, accompanied by Mr. Chew, both *en grande tenue*, to the Imperial Academy of Science, whose session was held to-day, the anniversary of its foundation. Ouvaroff, Minister of Public Construction, is President, and Prince Dondonkoff Korsakoff is Vice-President. I failed to catch precisely the name of the Secretary. The Metropolitan of Moscow, in full and very becoming pontifical robes, was present, and I had myself presented to him, being really unable to resist the benignity of his countenance and manner. We mutually regretted, through the medium of Korsakoff, our inability to speak any language understood by both. His mantle was of fine green cloth, and his mitre of white cassimere, with drapery falling behind and over his shoulders. In the centre of the front of his mitre was a brilliant diamond cross, and suspended from broad ribbons around his neck hung several rich crosses of great beauty. His beard was touched with gray and his moustache was long. I conjectured him to be about fifty, but was told he was more than seventy. The French Ambassador, the only *Chef* of the corps besides myself there, wore the uniform of the French National Institute,—a dark-green coat, embroidered with a lighter shade of green worsted in wreaths of laurel; it was otherwise strikingly plain, for I presume the cross on the left breast not to be part of the uniform. We were treated with two discourses. The first, by the Secretary, of great length, consuming no less than two hours in the reading, was an exposition of the doings of the institution during the last year, of the lives and characters of certain recently deceased members, and some interesting late discoveries and writings of the fraternity. Among others, the Secretary adverted to the singular result of an experiment with the galvanic battery by Yacobi, which I have heretofore noted; and he mentioned that the Academy had established with Dr. Herring, of New York, the means of exchanging the objects of natural science between the two countries. The second discourse was, unfortunately for me, in German; it was read by Mr. Behr, who enjoys a high reputation as a savant, and its subject was the classification of animals, showing the adaptation of their physical structure to the latitudes allotted for their residence. The Hall of the Academy was a very fine room, with lofty and painted ceilings, walls adorned with full-length portraits of the Emperor Paul, his Empress Marie, the Empress Catherine II., the Empress Elizabeth, and the Emperor Alexander, and the present Emperor, and the entablature, composed of a series of remarkably well-executed bass-reliefs, representing the employments of laborious industry. The upper end of the hall formed a large recess, supported by columns of beautiful marble, in the centre and front of which stood, on a dark greenish marble pedestal, a colossal bust of Peter the Great. The President, Vice-President, Secretary, and members, all in full dress of blue embroidered in gold, arranged themselves at a table which extended nearly the width of the room, covered with fine green cloth fringed with gold lace; the side of the table towards the audience was unoccupied. The meeting was thinly attended: hardly two hundred persons were present. Sir James Wylie, Admiral Krusenstern, and Admiral Rickards were there. I reached home a little before four P.M.

1839. *January* 13.—At half-past twelve (Sunday fairly over) went to the masquerade at the Great Theatre. All the Imperial family were present; the Empress and her daughter remaining as spectators seated in their box, while the Czar, the Grand Duke Michel, and Count Orloff seemed actively engaged among the crowd in the idle enjoyment of the scene. No hats are doffed on such occasions; nor does it seem expected that any more deference should be shown to the Sovereign than merely not to obstruct his path. He frequently had ladies, completely masked and disguised, on his arm, whom he obviously did not know, but with whom he was gayly jesting. Several times a lady would excite his curiosity to know who she was; and he summoned the Grand Duke Michel and Count Orloff to assist him in detecting her; but as the laws of the mask are never infringed, the trio, though uniting in comment and scrutiny and effort, did not appear to succeed. The costumes were not handsome or novel, and the masks were comparatively few. The amusement is a dull one, except to those who connect with it the irregularity and piquancy of intrigue; and they are probably very few.

1839. *January* 15.—We went at a quarter after nine in the evening to the British Embassy, at which the Corps Diplomatique generally assemble, and remained until two in the morning. There was dancing, at which I was favored with the hand of the French Ambassadress. The Marquis Clanricarde made himself unusually agreeable. He described Queen Victoria to me. She was a little lady, with large gray eyes that turned up impressively, and a peculiarity of bearing and manner which would make her remarked in any company. When she is gay, her joyousness is that of an open-faced girl, but the instant she is serious, she draws down the corners of her mouth, drops her eyes, and looks intent. She sings well and reads admirably, filling the largest hall with a voice and enunciation as distinct as a bell, without the least exertion.

1839. *January* 20.—Interesting public events are happening on several great theatres. In France, the ministry of Count Molé is being driven out by a coalition between the respective parties of Guizot, Thiers, and Odillon Barrot, aided by the ultra-Legitimists, and this at a moment when the country is wonderfully prosperous and the successful bombardment of the castle of San Juan de Ulua is being proclaimed. It is obvious that matters cannot stand still in France; and the Hollando-Belgic question may be, after all, the safest vent for an explosion which may otherwise overwhelm the dynasty of Louis Philippe and create a general war of the two principles. France is actually a mercurial democracy, whose start may be hourly expected. In England, the working classes are suffering from want of food, and are assuming the calm attitude of an inflexible purpose. The arrest of Stephens on a charge of sedition is calculated to concentrate and harmonize their efforts. The corn-laws cannot be yielded to the popular clamour without a resort to other than land taxes for the payment of the interest on the public debt. The recent Poor Law appears excessively odious. In the midst of the excitements flowing from these causes, it is apparent that a vigorous republican spirit is rising, that the monarchy, with its girl as chief, is falling into contempt, and that a change of ministry is at hand. The example of the French opposition will probably be followed by the Whigs and Tories, of whom a coalition will be patched up to resist both the precursorship of O'Connell and the radical Chartists. Such a coalition, however, will be deemed so unprincipled and detestable that it must occasion scenes of violence everywhere. We must have the Manchester murders repeated before long. The cry of " No popery!" too, is getting up, and with really more reason than existed in Lord George Gordon's time. The civil war in Spain is becoming too barbarous to be interesting, nor does there seem on either side the capacity to bring it to an end: endless and useless butcheries of defenceless prisoners; unceasing changes of the ministry; a wretched lack of money; a total destitution of talent, political or military.

1839. *January* 23.—Visited and made the personal acquaintance of the once-celebrated songstress, Mademoiselle Sontag, now Countess Rossi. She is pretty,—a round face, fine large white teeth, clear and delicate complexion, blue eyes, and brown hair.

A ball at the British clergyman's, Mr. Law's, with card-playing and supper, immediately under the church! Did not get through it all until three in the morning. Dreadful in every aspect!

1839. *January* 26.—I dined to-day with Sir James Wiley, and was agreeably surprised by meeting the following mixed company: Count Nesselrode, Marquis Clanricarde, Prince Mensikoff, Count Volkonsky, Count Kreptovitch, Count Matuzevitch, Mr. Poletica, Prince ——, Mr. ——, Mr. Hodgson, Mr. Law, Mr. Plinkey, Mr. Cayley, Mr. Nichols, Mr. Gray, Mr. Maberly, etc. I had not before seen, except once at the *public* table of the English Club, this union of high nobility with high merchants and shopkeepers. Sir James told me that the Emperor Alexander had delineated with his own hands the coat-of-arms he assigned for him at the time he made him a knight. His knighthood was authorized and confirmed by his English sovereign.

1839. *January* 28.—Dined with Mr. Hodgson at half-past five. Sir James Wylie, Sir Edward Baynes, Mr. Buchanan, Mr. Edwards, Mr. Atkinson, Mr. Krehmer, Mr. Grant, etc. Sir James Wylie was at a loss to know why, as he had been very intimate with John D. Lewis at that time, he had not formed my acquaintance when I was here many years ago. I suggested that he was then probably with the Russian armies in Germany, and asked him where he was when Moreau was killed at Dresden. "Close by him," was the reply, "and I amputated both his legs at the thighs." He then gave me, with his usual garrulity, a long and not uninteresting account of the particulars of that well-known event. Moreau's first exclamation to him was, "Qu'il est facheux, mon cher Docteur, que ce misérable (Napoleon) m'a attrapé ici." They were obliged to move him about a good deal in order to get him into a place of safety, but Sir James thinks that the operation had been so fortunate that he would have survived had not Metternich and the Duke of Cumberland (now King of Hanover) thrown him into a fever by prolonged political conversations. He died on the thirteenth day after being wounded, at a village called, I think, Drux. His body was embalmed and sent to this city.

1839. *February* 1.—Lord Clanricarde has experienced latterly a series of little *contretemps* which are the subjects of conversation, and are calculated to worry him. Several gentlemen invited him to join them on a hunt. They went to Oranienbaum, an estate of the Grand Duke Michel. While sporting, the party were met by the keeper, who required them to produce their authorizations. The only ticket in the possession of one of them was insufficient, and they were ordered off and their game taken from them. His lordship returned to St. Petersburg indignant and mortified. When the matter was communicated to the Grand Duchess Helen, she immediately directed a party to be got up for the special amusement of the Ambassador, and the whole estate to be at his disposal for the occasion. Having had his sport, he applied by note to the Grand Master of Ceremonies to be permitted to thank her Imperial Highness in person. This note remained unanswered for four days. He was again indignant and mortified, and went to his friend General Tschitcherine. The General spoke to the Grand Duchess, who exclaimed at her own forgetfulness, but said, "Never mind; we will put the thing right by giving the Embassy a special *soirée* to-morrow night." This was done. Then the Marquis invited the Grand Duke to come to his house this evening, and, in further reconciliation, the Grand Duke did so. But, unfortunately, the Marquis does not know the established rule of etiquette here, that he who invites an Imperial personage to his house must devote himself exclusively to that personage; and it happened, still more unfortunately, that on the arrival of the Grand Duke, the Ambassador was dancing, so that his Imperial Highness did not receive the customary attention, and went away again in less than half an hour. The string of mischances did not end here. There was a large supper, at which all the guests were seated. Of course, the signal for rising could be given only by the Ambassador and Ambassadress; yet, after a while, as if by a preconcerted plan, nearly all the company rose, and hurried away, leaving the Marquis and his lady, with about ten others, still eating. He is again mortified and indignant.

1839. *February* 4.—Went to a *soirée dansante et musicale* at Princess Hohenlohe's. It was principally composed of members of the Diplomatic Corps. We remained till two in the morning. The French Ambassador answered my inquiries about Berryer, whose "paroles foudroyantes" in the Chamber of Deputies produced so much effect in the recent discussion, by saying that he was as a mere orator unrivalled,—he is a lawyer, fine figure, fine action, powerful voice,—but that as a statesman his opinions or speeches went very little way. Miss Youchkoff's execution on the piano was good. We had several admirable songs, particularly a duet. Countess Rossi scrupulously avoided coming until all the music was over, as it is understood she will not sing publicly. The mazourka degenerated into a romp under the auspices of Lord Clanricarde, who was quite overcome with laughter at the accidents encountered by his attaché, young Wombwell.

1839. *February* 13.—This being Carnival, and the common sports in full blast on the square fronting the Admiralty, Philip and I started at noon on an exploration expedition. We were detained, however, nearly two hours in the large theatre erected, witnessing rope-dancing and harlequin transformations. Things were rather too coarse for our taste, and we pursued the hunt no farther.

1839. *February* 15.—The Carnival sports on the Admiralty Square are becoming crowded and lively. The ice hills appear the principal objects of attraction, and are in constant activity. The procession of equipages, to-day, was more than usually long and brilliant. I counted twenty handsome carriages in succession, drawn by six horses, with coachman, postilion, and servant in cocked hat and rich scarlet liveries. These are the pupils of the Imperial institution devoted to the education of the daughters of the nobility. The number of drunken men in the streets hourly increases.

Louis Philippe is unwilling to part with Count Molé. Marshal Soult is too ill or too much puzzled to form a fresh ministry, and the French Chambers are first prorogued and then dissolved! Spirits appear to me so much excited in Paris, and the general tendency of things so strong for change, that one may anticipate serious events. The King must *govern* now decidedly, or will soon cease to *reign*.

1839. *February* 23.—The Emperor is reported unwell. On Monday last he reviewed some troops at Peterhoff, and, while riding over a plain, his horse sunk so deeply in the snow that he was obliged to dismount and walk. The snow got into his boots and wet his feet thoroughly. He neglected the circumstance. On Tuesday he complained, and on Wednesday, a fever coming on, he sent for his physician. He came to St. Petersburg yesterday, and is said to be better. Among the court flies one can perceive great solicitude, accompanied by an effort to make light of the attack. It is impossible not to speculate upon the vast consequences which would immediately result to Russia and to Europe by the sudden death of this sovereign. His heir is at Naples. The Empress has no political talent or taste. The Grand Duke Michel is beloved by the army. The Duke of Leuchtenberg is not yet married.

1839. *February 27.*—At half-past ten A.M. I drove to the Church of St. Alexander Neffsky, to attend, agreeably to invitation, the funeral of Count Speransky, President of the Legislative Department of the Imperial Council, who died on Saturday last. The Ambassadors of Austria and France were the only other members of the diplomatic body present. The Emperor and Grand Duke Michel were there, the former seeming in some degree to divide the attention of the officiating priests. The loss of Speransky is represented as a severe one to the country. He was remarkable for ability. He had experienced great vicissitudes of fortune; was at one time banished to Siberia, upon the false charge of having secretly furnished Napoleon with the drafts of certain Russian fortifications. He had many inveterate enemies among the nobles, in consequence of his plans for ameliorating the condition of the boors. He subsequently became Governor-General of Siberia. He died after a short illness.

His death produces a succession of official changes. Daschkoff, the Minister of Justice, takes his place in the Imperial Council; my friend Bloudoff replaces Daschkoff, and Gournieff, Bloudoff. This is rotation without promotion.

Prince Hohenlohe, who, with the Princess, her sister, Madame Youchkoff, and Miss Youchkoff, spent the *avant-soirée* with us, says that there is great activity just now in the department of Foreign Affairs here, and that couriers are despatching in all directions. As the Belgian question would seem quietly inurned, this bustle cannot well be explained, except by referring it to an alleged communication of Lord Clanricarde to Count Nesselrode, to the effect that England would no longer put up with the interference of Russia in her relations with Persia, and that if they were continued war would be the consequence.

Prince Hohenlohe told me the following anecdote: Some ten or twelve years ago, Jerome Bonaparte, now called Count de Montfort, at a *soirée* of his own, played cards with great vehemence. He lost all the money he had about him, then pledged his rings, and finally laid his watch upon the table. It was a small gold one, the back of which opened by a spring. A lady, overlooking the game, admired the watch, and took it up to examine. On her attempting to open the back, Jerome immediately clasped it, and said that must not be done. His wife, who stood by, insisted upon knowing what was in it; grew angry, reproached him with having some keepsake of a favorite there, and finally, bursting into tears, quit the room. Jerome then opened the watch, showed to all present that it contained a beautiful miniature of his first wife (Betsey Paterson), with the remark, "You see, I hope, that I could not with propriety let her look at it." The Prince says that it was notorious that he remained deeply attached to his first wife long after their separation.

1839. *March* 6.—Sigismund Thalberg gave his first concert in St. Petersburg this evening at the "Assemblée de la Noblesse." I had obtained four tickets out of the nine hundred sold, which were at fifteen roubles, or three dollars per ticket. We went half an hour earlier than the appointed time, in order to get convenient seats, but we found the saloon already crowded. Many had gone as early as five in the afternoon, to wait patiently till eight. Everybody of ton and distinction was there, and the Imperial box was graced by the three Grand Duchesses, Helen, Marie, and Olga, attended by Baroness Fredericks and Kitty Tschitcherine.

A great poet, a great orator, a great painter, and a great musician (composer as well as performer) are scarcely to be separated on the scale of intellectual power and interest. Thalberg is the first musical genius I have ever seen. I had anticipated much, but he more than satisfied me. He executed on the piano three of his own pieces, and made the instrument speak in tones I never imagined it capable of. The vast and discerning audience testified in tumults of applause to his triumph. He seems a young man of twenty-five, of rather slender figure, florid complexion, light-chestnut hair, and a distinct Grecian profile. His personal deportment was modest, deferential, but perfectly self-composed and calm. Dressed in full black, with white cravat, and maintaining a mild but imperturbable serenity, he took his seat at the piano with the preoccupied air of a young clergyman full of his first interesting sermon. His first touch carried conviction of his excellence. It involved a delicacy, a certainty, an entirety, which made the note fall in its utmost perfection upon the ear. As he proceeded, this exquisite distinctness accompanied him through all the mazes of his elaborated composition. The instrument seemed like a wonderful combination of the richest, clearest, and sweetest human voices.

In coming away, the sudden rush through the antechambers was rather alarming. We got, however, in the advance group with Count Nesselrode (whose little rake-hat made him look as if he had already been squeezed to death, and who kept screaming for his weeping and terrified daughter Marie), Princess Soltikoff, Countess Kreptovitch, etc., and were able to reach our carriage with no mishap, except the loss of a breastpin.

1839. *March* 12.—At half-past ten we went to Princess Hohenlohe's, and remained till half-past two. I played chess with the representative of Don Carlos, the Duke of Medina-Sidonia and Marquis of Villafranca; giving him a castle and a knight, and then beating him. The company was numerous and gay. Thalberg made his appearance as a guest, and seemed very much courted by some of the younger married ladies. He declines playing at such parties, unless engaged for the purpose, and then his fixed price is one thousand roubles, or two hundred dollars, for the evening, during which he executes two or three pieces. Hohenlohe is not up to such extravagance; but the pianist finds himself in pretty constant demand. What orator, statesman, lawyer, poet, or even novelist has ever been paid at this rate?

Galignani mentions a musician, now in London, whose

name I forget, who demands for private concerts a compensation of two hundred and fifty pounds, or one thousand one hundred and eleven dollars a night, and, what's more, he gets it!

1839. *March* 14.—At half-past four went with Mrs. Dallas to the splendid dinner of Prince Youssoupoff. There were about fifty guests. The extent of this palace and the magnificence of its furniture and arrangements struck us as forcibly as ever. The Prince has his band of music (the only private one of which I am aware), and it played at a short distance from the company, changing its position when the dinner was announced, during the whole of the entertainment. He has also a theatre attached to the establishment; and his household servants number five hundred. There were present the French Ambassador and Madame, Count and Countess Benkendorf, Prince Mentchikoff, Baron and Baroness Fredericks, Prince and Princess Hohenlohe, Count and Countess Rossi, Countess Modené, Prince and Princess Sherbatoff, Madame Paliansky, Baron Seebach, Mr. Soltikoff, Mr. Bloudoff, Mr. Polycarpoff, several ladies whose names I did not know, and a number of military officers. Count Bobrinsky, my landlord, was there; and having ascertained, by an experience of eighteen months, that I was not disposed to make the slightest advance towards his acquaintance, he sought a personal introduction. On the score of character and intelligence, he stands very high. I sat at table between Prince Mentchikoff and Madame Paliansky, both of whom were agreeable; the Minister of the Marine very shy about the actual condition and number of the Russian navy, and the lady amazed to hear of a country in which husbands were faithful to their wives. She thought she would send her daughters to marry in America. Mrs. Dallas, placed between Baron Fredericks and Mr. Bloudoff, was as fortunate as myself in having conversable neighbours. The dinner was excellent, especially in the last glass of wine circulated, which was "Cape" or Constantia, of a hundred years of age.

1839. *March* 15.—At eight P.M. we repaired to the Theatre Michel to witness "Un grand concert, vocal et instrumental, avec des Tableaux-Vivans." The music was not much. The tableaux were the finest we had seen on a large scale, and, being managed very effectively, pleased us exceedingly. They were sixteen in number: 1. Lady Percy; 2. Constance and Prince Arthur; 3. Don Juan and Haidee; 4. Aboul Cassem and Dardone; 5. Que voulez-vous? 6. Passez votre chemin; 7. Le repos du soldat; 8. La danse de la Gitana; 9. Le bon vin de Gordon; 10. Le brigand de nuit; 11. Le désastre de famille; 12. Les maux des dents; 13. Le coup de vent; 14. L'homme qui se nage; 15. The Devil; 16. Une fille mal gardée. Of these the 8th and the 16th were the largest and most striking. It was said that these tableaux are sometimes indelicate. On the present occasion, nothing could be more correct.

Adjourning from the Theatre at eleven o'clock we went to Countess Modené's, and remained for nearly two hours. Nothing could be kinder or more after our own taste than the domestic reception given to us. The old lady took to her game of whist with Baron Schleinitz, while her three daughters, Madame Paschkoff, Princess Shakoffsky, and an unmarried one called Marie, conversed and entertained. The green arbours and rich flowers arranged about the rooms were beautiful. I sat in one of the arbours illuminated by a Chinese lamp and beat Princess Shakoffsky two rapid games of chess. Our only refreshment was an excellent cup of tea.

1839. *March* 16.—I went, agreeably to special invitation, to join the dinner-celebration of the anniversary of the English Club. Count Cancrin was chairman or presiding officer, and, being stationed at his side, I inquired as to the new process which I understood had been discovered for separating gold from silver in the ore. He told me that it was the discovery of a Frenchman at Paris, to whom they had been obliged to pay one hundred and twenty thousand francs for communicating it; and that its principal merit consists in the improvement of the machinery used. It had, however, not yet been definitely tested here. He told me that the mines in Siberia might be considered as yielding five hundred pounds of gold per annum, or eighteen thousand English pounds, and that they were enlarging and improving. They employed thirty thousand persons, who received a monthly compensation, varying from, the lowest, fifteen roubles to forty or fifty.

At nine in the evening we went to a musical and *soirée* at Madame Polycarpoff's. The great object of attraction and source of infinite gratification was the celebrated composer and pianist, Henselt, who played on the instrument for nearly two hours, in a style that quite equalled, if it did not surpass, Thalberg. He is said to be the natural son of the present King of Bavaria, and is about twenty-five years of age. He is an enthusiast in his art, and while performing seems to become perfectly intoxicated with the sounds he produces. His fingering was peculiar and rather disagreeable to the eye,—his hand, a dead white, seeming to lie flat on the keys, and the fingers to roll over each other like worms or leeches. Occasionally he struck with a force which the instrument could scarcely resist long. He gives nine lessons a day, at twenty roubles the lesson, and his public concerts are always overflowing. It is now something more than a year since his arrival in St. Petersburg.

1839. March 17.—In the evening, at half-past ten, Mrs. Dallas accompanied me to Count Nesselrode's. The Countess has been absent for three or four weeks, and we were in duty bound to welcome her return. The Ambassadors (except the British, who is still confined to a dark room with a gouty affection of the eye) and the Diplomatic Corps generally were there. I had an interesting conversation with General Kissilieff, who is highly esteemed for his administrative ability, and Barante. The former alleged that there were not more than two or three Russian merchants in St. Petersburg, that foreign commerce was wholly in the hands of resident strangers, and he described the course of it as what we would consider a mere commission business. Hence he concluded that, though now and then failures might occur to some extent, there could be no general bankruptcy, no pervading crisis, such as seems to happen almost periodically in the United States, Great Britain, and France. Barante thought otherwise, and, without explaining the grounds of his opinion, predicted an early and violent derangement of trade here. Both these gentlemen seemed to ascribe the recent calamity of the United States to the inconceivable number and gambling tendency of our banks. Neither of them could understand why the American people were so averse to a national bank, which, as they said, centralized the financial power; and it was vain for me to tell them that, however important and attractive this very centralization might be in France or Russia, in America it was inconsistent with some fundamental principles, dangerous as a lever, and repugnant to sentiments which were general when the government was created, and which have since been confirmed by experience. Having got the fixed European idea that we are wholly a commercial people, they argue that whatever spurs and facilitates commerce must be a primary object with us.

1839. *March* 19.—At half-past ten I went alone to Princess Hohenlohe's rout. The company was unusually crowded and brilliant. The Grand Duke Michel took the extraordinary trouble to come up and converse with me. As I have never shown the slightest disposition to court his Imperial Highness, in the manner so customary among the best here, and as that sort of courtship is deemed necessary to the slightest favour or notice, I was as much surprised at his volunteer as he professed to be at my capital French. He was tired of his effort before I well got over my astonishment. I am no admirer of the Grand Duke. Played chess with the French Ambassador; beat the first and lost the second game.

1839. *March* 23.—I have repeatedly met the Emperor walking alone on the English Quay lately. He looks thinner, and has less colour than usual. He invariably stops to shake hands and to make some commonplace remark. To-day he made me walk a little with him, and spoke feelingly of the recent illness of the Empress, whom he called, in imitation of plain republican language, "*my wife*." He spoke English. His manner of walking is ungraceful, bending at his knees too much, and swinging his arms from the elbows too actively.

The Princess Shakoffsky, who spent the *avant-soirée* with us, gave an animated account of the recent Persian Ambassador at this court. He was a young man, scarcely one-and-twenty. He dressed in the rich and multifarious costume of his own country, with a number of what we would call "morning gowns," which he would often remove, one by one, as he felt himself, while visiting, getting too warm. He could not bear to see ladies and gentlemen dancing together, considering it offensive to modesty, and at balls kept his eyes studiously upon the floor; and yet he esteemed all women as mere objects of sale; and on one occasion, at the theatre, struck by the extraordinary beauty of the Countess Zavadowski, he sent round to inquire at what price she could be purchased. He was passionately devoted to chess, and obliged the young men of his suite to play with him, and always to be beaten, morning, noon, and night. Once, at a large party, Princess Shakoffsky challenged him to a game. He seemed to think it impossible for a lady to have any skill. She asked him whether she was bound not to win finally. He replied that he would not play unless she promised to exert herself to conquer; and they began. In a short time she checked his king and queen, and took the latter. He became excessively agitated, and summoned to his assistance his four secretaries, who became themselves apparently much disquieted. The company clustered round the board, and took sides, and the Princess received so much and such various advice as to each move, that she ceased to think for herself, and lost the game. Early next morning she was waited upon by the four secretaries, who believed she had purposely lost the game, and who came to thank her, as, had she won it, they would probably have undergone imprisonment for a month! He was in the practice of walking about with his eyes shut or bandaged, saying that he wanted to accustom himself to live and move without seeing, as he presumed he should one day be deprived of his vision. Since his return to Persia, for some real or supposed offence, he has had his eyes torn out.

1839. *March* 23.—We spent the evening at Madame Paschkoff's, meeting her mother, La Marquise, and another old and chatty personage. These ladies complain of the practice recently adopted by governments of frequently changing their diplomatic representatives at their Court. In former times, they say, Ministers remained twenty, thirty, and even forty years, and they formed firm friendships. Now one is shy in making diplomatic acquaintances, fearing an early and abrupt close to them. Certainly ever since my coming the changes have been numerous. There were several other ladies, Madame Lanskoy, her daughter, and some young gentlemen. The little *maigre* supper, introduced at half-past eleven, was extremely nice, consisting of fish dressed in five or six different ways,—one slightly soused, another *en papillotte*, with minced mushrooms, a third " *à la befstik*," a fourth fried with smelts, etc. During the last week of the carème they are not allowed even fish, and live upon mushrooms, potatoes, and leavened bread. The room in which we sat was adorned with fine and blooming flowers, among which I noticed a rich white lilac, and the voice of a nightingale seemed to fill up all conversational pauses.

1839. *March* 24.—The average annual quantity of the famous Russian leather, called *youfta*, exported during the years from 1834 to 1837 was 66,637 ponds, or 2,398,932 pounds, in 159,591 pieces. The exportation annually diminishes as the manufacture of leather improves in other countries. More than half the amount exported goes into the different states of Europe.

1839. *March* 25.—The "Incidents of Travel in Russia," by I. L. Stevens, of New York, has amused me greatly. It is light and superficial, but gay and natural. In general his descriptions of St. Petersburg are faithful. He exaggerates a little for effect. Thus, he represents the *Admiralty* as having "a façade of marble, with ranges of columns a quarter of a mile in length." Now, there is *no* marble; about four dozen brick-red plaster columns, and the length is about one-half the supposed extent. "The Winter Palace is a gigantic and princely structure, built of marble." Certainly gigantic and princely, but *not* built of marble. "The marble palace built by Catherine II. for her favourite, Prince Orloff, with a basement of granite and superstructure of bluish marble, ornamented with marble columns and pillars," has no marble about it, but reddish pilasters of rather a mean appearance, and the blue is scant and mean. The "great Church of St. Isaac, of marble, jasper, and porphyry, upon a *foundation of granite*," will certainly be one of the wonders of art when finished; and, though its basement be granite, its foundation is unfortunately of piles, and serious fears are entertained that it will sink, as its predecessor did, owing to the enormous weight placed upon the unsteady earth.

1839. *March* 26.—At seven, Mrs. Dallas, Julia, Elizabeth, and I repaired to the grand concert given by the Society of Patriotic Ladies for the benefit of their schools. These ladies had sent me two tickets, and I procured two others through the politeness of Count Wielnorski. For the four I paid one hundred roubles. On reaching the magnificent hall, the Salle de la Noblesse, we found it crammed with about fifteen hundred visitors; but seats had been set apart for the Diplomatic Corps, which we managed to attain by passing across the elevated platform appropriated to the music, to the opposite side of the room, very nearly *en face* of the Imperial box. Nothing could exceed the splendour of the scene. All that is noble and fashionable and elegant and tasty were assembled, the military and ladies richly dressed. The whole of the Imperial family (except the Grand Duchess Helen, who is unwell) were present. The Empress, Marie, and Olga, clothed in white, their foreheads glittering with diamonds, with the two boy Grand Dukes, Baroness Fredericks, and Prince Volkonsky, were stationed, like the gorgeous figures of a superb tableau, in the crimson-velvet lined and curtained recess, or rather small room, just in front of us, while the Emperor and Grand Duke Michel found their way at an open door close by, and stood tranquilly in the crowd. Here were certainly at a *coup d'œil* to be seen the *élite* of St. Petersburg, if not of all Russia. All the dames and demoiselles d'honneur, and ladies of distinction, occupied the first ten or twelve benches nearest the music. All the general officers, with their dazzling epaulettes and swords, were clustered about, standing. All the Imperial Council, and the Senate, and the État Major were collected. Nobody seemed to be absent whose presence could add to the brilliant *tout ensemble*. The Ambassadors of Austria, France, and England, the British Ambassadress, the Prussian, Dutch, and Sardinian Ministers, the Saxon, Swedish, and Bavarian chargés, Mademoiselle Barante and her brother, the secretaries d'Andre, Edwardes, Kaizenfelds, and attachés d'Appony,

Vrints, Wombwell, young Roger Schimmelpenninck, Count Nesselrode, Count Woronzow, Count Levarchaff, Count Wassiltchickoff, General Kissilief, Count Montcillo, Mrs. Dallas, Julia, Elizabeth, and myself constituted what might be esteemed the group of the diplomatic section. The concert, which takes place annually, is one of the contributions of the nobility to charitable purposes. Its performances are executed by the most disguished ladies, and the instruments are managed chiefly by amateur gentlemen. Countess Annette Benkendorff, the daughter of the present Governor of the city, and a young lady whose loveliness would be irresistible but for a most atrocious squint; Madame Krudener, decidedly the recognized beauty and a great favourite; and Madame Bartinieff, a dame d'honneur in high favour, were the three most conspicuous of the Russian ladies, aided by thirty or forty others who formed a line with them on the platform and joined in the singing. At the head, however, of the songstresses was the magnet of the evening, the celebrated and incomparable Sontag, now Countess Rossi. She had been persuaded to run the risk of reviving past recollections, to forget that she had stepped from the boards of the opera into the rank of a minister and the arms of a Count, and to lead the flower of Russian noblesse and fashion on this benevolent occasion. What a splendid triumph did a single gift of nature seem to obtain! Her voice overwhelmed competition, and by its wonderful volume and sweetness produced a sort of enchantment which made you for a while insensible to anything else. The Czar, his Court and his Army, all seemed to lose their *prestige* and their power while that magical voice dominated the ear. She sang twice, first the finale of Donizetti's opera, "Anna Bolena," and

was in this accompanied by Madame Bartinieff and
Madame Krudener and three gentlemen; second, Bellini's "Norma." The effect of the last song was beyond
description, and the applause was vehement and protracted. It recalled Malibran to my mind, and yet
seemed superior by the addition to her voice of that of
her father, Garcia. Nothing could be richer, nothing
could be clearer, nothing could be vaster, nothing could
be softer, nothing could be deeper, nothing could be
more delicate, and nothing could be more decided. I
might go on multiplying epithets without describing a
bit more distinctly. On the whole, I think it was the
best singing I ever heard, and as good as can be. The
manner of the Countess was perhaps a little constrained
in the effort to avoid relapsing into the cantatrice, and on
two occasions, instead of confining her courtesy to the
Empress, she for an instant bent to the applauding audience. I doubt much whether this taste of the glory of
past times was not more really delightful to her than any
of the rank or other results of her marriage. She was
sent for by the Empress at the close of her song, an act
which is the common courtesy shown to professional
songsters, and which has been constantly shown to
Taglioni,—I thought the discriminating delicacy of her
Majesty might have avoided on this occasion.

1839. *April* 4.—Received a notification from the
Master of Ceremonies of a Court Circle to be held in
the *Winter Palace!* on Tuesday next.

The discreditable practice of opening letters as they
pass through the Post-Office—a practice said to be universal, and of which I have had convincing proofs—is
attested by several anecdotes current here, of which I
note the two following. Not long ago one of the For-

eign Ministers complained in person to Count Nesselrode that he had received a bundle of despatches through the Post-Office, rumpled, torn, and obviously having been opened. The Count coolly observed, "It must have been done very carelessly: I will give instructions against such negligence in future." On another occasion, the Swedish Minister, meeting the Director-General of the Post-Office, casually said to him that his subordinates ought to be more careful in their process of examining his letters; the Director gravely protested that nothing of the sort was done. "Oh, I don't mind it," said the Baron; "but as in their hurry they sent me my despatches from Stockholm with the seal of the Minister of Foreign Affairs of Holland, I think they want lecturing." The Director only replied with the exclamation, " Is it possible ?"

1839. *April 7.*—This being the Russian Easter, all the churches were crowded at midnight to perform the ceremony of welcoming it. The Imperial Court and high priesthood assembled in the Winter Palace, Mass is said; the clergy circulate in their numerous chapels as if to search for the buried Christ; they retire behind the doors, and at a particular moment the holy doors fly open, when the priests in their fullest costume proclaim to the people, with exultation, "Christ is risen!" All the church-bells are immediately in full chorus, salutes of artillery are fired, and everybody embraces his neighbour with the enthusiastic outcry, "Christ is risen!" The uproar seemed to be prolonged until three o'clock this morning. The ensuing week is the liveliest carnival.

1839. *April 10.*—The reoccupation of the *Winter Palace* has been signalized by splendid "*gratifications*" from the Emperor to those who have contributed to its reconstruction. General Klein-Mehel has received a *loan* of one million of roubles with which to purchase an estate, and the Order of St. Andrew, with a gold medal surrounded by brilliants. Count Cernicheff received as a gift three hundred thousands roubles, and it is supposed will be sent Ambassador to Vienna, a post for which Benkendorff and Clien-Mehel are his competitors. All the subordinate labourers on the Palace have received silver medals, and now parade them on their breasts at the Cachelles. At this season of every year it is customary to distribute more or less of these Imperial favours.

The mortality among the workmen engaged in rebuilding the Winter Palace is represented to have been frightful. As the Emperor had undertaken to re-enter during the feasts of Easter, immense heat was kept up in the interior to dry the walls, etc., and this produced all sorts of fatal disorders. Of course, this effect of his will was not communicated to his Majesty.

1839. *April* 14.—The Court Circle, intended to have been held at the Winter Palace on Tuesday last, was deferred, owing to the fatigue and indisposition of the Empress, to this day, at noon. I reached the Diplomatic reception-room without traversing much of the residue of this magnificent, newly-finished structure. The basement affords accommodations for any crowds of servants; and the white marble stairway leading to the upper story, with its lofty, painted, and gilded ceiling, and its ornamental statuary, is vast, striking, and beautiful. The apartment assigned to the Foreign Ministers was one in which a small and handsome throne occupied the centre of a large recess, immediately in front of a painting of Peter the Great guided by Wisdom; its walls were of crimson velvet studded with gold double-headed eagles somewhat larger than a man's hand; from the vaulted ceiling hung the richest and tastiest chandelier of solid silver, chased and worked into oak-wreaths encircling Russian eagles, the immense size of which surprised me; against the walls a number of lustres of the same rich and solid material, each six or eight feet high, exquisitely elaborated, were attached, and in two piers stood wide tables of pure silver. The mixture of gold and silver, though it seemed to increase the gorgeous display, detracted from the taste of the ensemble. The steps and floor of the platform on which the throne stood were carpeted with rich crimson velvet; the rest of the floor was figured and waxed wood.

1839. *April* 15.—I procured tickets for the admission of my family to explore the Winter Palace, and we repaired thither at one o'clock. We entered by the great central door on the river-side and mounted the noble marble staircase, whose solid, carved, and polished banisters of the same material particularly struck us. We travelled rather too rapidly through this vast building; except the quarters designed for the Duke and Duchess of Leuchtenberg, and some of the largest halls or saloons, especially that of St. George, not yet quite finished, we visited in succession the great saloons of State, and of banquet, and of dance, the Imperial Chapel and the private Chapel of the Emperor, the " *Salle des Marechaux,*" the suite of private apartments appropriated to the Empress, another suite appropriated to the Czar, another suite to the Grand Duchesses Marie and Olga, another suite to the Grand Duke Héritier, another suite to the younger sons, and an infinite variety of halls, antechambers, corridors, and galleries, which cannot be particularly designated. In surveying the endless elaboration of work of all kinds bestowed upon this building, one is utterly at a loss to comprehend how it could be executed by human means in the course of the brief interval between the conflagration and the present moment. An exclamation to this effect involuntarily escapes the lips as you enter each one of the more important chambers. The Imperial Chapel alone, with its minute and various carving and gilding, would seem to have necessarily exacted more time. Every department of art, from its humblest to its highest region,—architecture, painting, sculpture; all the mechanic arts; the working in gold, in silver, in brass, in iron, in glass, in all sorts of woods and stones and cloths,—with the heads to arrange and direct, and the arms to procure and fashion and fasten material, must have been put under high steam pressure without abatement or cessation. Nothing more exquisitely luxurious, costly, and refined can be imagined than the private apartments of the Empress. They remind one of the descriptions in Lalla Rookh, of the Moorish Alhambra, of Sardanapalus, and of the Arabian Nights. Her parlour, with its ponderous golden doors, pilasters of malachite, screens of cut glass variously coloured, arched ceiling beautifully painted, and corresponding furniture and ornaments; her bedroom, with its coverlid, an entire piece of point lace about ten feet square, reposing on a sky-blue satin bed, and its toilet-table with more than a hundred elegantly shaped and worked vessels and mirror frames, all of massive gold; her Turkish bath-room, with its soft, deep, impalpable carpet, its fantastic walls, its fount, its shell-reservoir, its white marble basin, and its adjoining mirrors; her elysian bower, with the vast sunken bath, and its white marble walls and stairway, and its jet d'eau in the centre, with flowers and shrubbery ever blooming and fragrant around; her rose-coloured tea-room, which seems to the eye like a bouquet of delicate roses; her family sitting-room, with the miniatures of her husband and children fastened to screens that encircle lounges, and the thousand knickknackeries of precious stones, and the delicious paintings of Raphael, and the carved ivory boxes, and the beautiful full-length statue of herself in one corner: all these and many additional may be noted, but cannot be described except in the poetical language of Tom Moore, Washington Irving, or Lord Byron. There was a striking and agreeable difference between these apartments and those of the Autocrat. In the latter, nothing was feminine, everything elegant, commodious, nothing useless or trifling. He has no bed, he has no carpets, he has no toilet-table, he has no knickknackery. Such also were the rooms of the Grand Duke. The Grand Duchess's, on the contrary, partook of the delicacy and luxury of the Empress's. I noticed that his Majesty has transferred Horace Vernet's Review by Napoleon from the Hermitage to a corner of one of his private apartments. The two paintings by Vanloo, in the principal parlour of the Duchess Marie, are exceedingly well selected and beautiful. We penetrated into the room assigned as the sanctuary of the Imperial crown jewels through immense folding-doors of iron; but the glass cases in their golden frames were patiently and in emptiness waiting for their destined contents. In the chambers of the younger children was a room provided with a small sentry-box, two small muskets, and the posts used in front of guard-houses as props for arms: this is the military closet of the two Grand Dukes. In one of the rooms of the

Empress I was pleased with the apparent lightness and finish of the sofas, chairs, and tables; they were of iron, highly polished, and looking like the most fragile ebony.

1839. *April* 17.—No stranger can pretend to ascertain with any certainty the military forces of this Empire. Official records (the only sure proof) are, of course, locked in impenetrable mystery. Conversation with the highest functionaries on the subject is never otherwise than vague and speculative. Most of them are intentionally kept ignorant, and the very few who really do know something about the matter with precision, deem the details of a nature to justify their being wary and evasive. Generally, there is an obvious tendency to exaggerate the number of the army and navy; but, at the largest estimate I have heard or seen, the Russian army is not such as to warrant the impression that prevails through Europe and elsewhere of the colossal power of the nation. Let us see.

The most overrated accounts represent the Russian military—that is, the organized regular army—as exceeding a million. I do not doubt its being at least eight hundred thousand. Is this enough to make Russia a permanently formidable and dangerous power? It should be recollected that an army is only formidable to other countries as it may be moved and directed abroad. If it cannot quit home, however strong for protection it may be, it is nothing that need be feared. Now, the government of this vast Empire, in all its ramifications, is conducted by and through its army; the whole machine is an encampment. The police is military; the collection of the revenue is military; the public institutions of all kinds, which are very numerous, are under the care of the military; the mint, the banks, the great schools, the palaces, and Imperial estates are in the management and custody of the military. So much of the army as is thus engaged is without the power of locomotion; there is nothing to take its place and perform its duties as a substitute, even for the shortest time; there is not and *cannot be anything like a militia*. To maintain civil government, then, at home must exact the constant presence of a large proportion of the million. Then, again, there are certain duties universally regarded as of a strictly military character which, nevertheless, divide, weaken, and keep stationary another large proportion. The frontiers are extensive, and must be guarded; the colonies require fixed protection; the garrisons, forts, arsenals, war academies, foundries, etc., must be kept going. If to these considerations you add the broad and practical necessity of securing a despotism against popular conspiracies and frenzies, by an unceasing display of bayonets and troops, what becomes of the lofty-sounding and dread-inspiring million of soldiers? I should say that three-fourths of them, however effective for domestic purposes, are nothing, perhaps worse than nothing, in relation to their capacity to do mischief abroad. Even for defence, they are not comparable to our million and a half of militia, simply because, according to the existing system, they must everywhere discharge essential municipal duties, and are thus incompetent to movability or concentration.

Taking the million, therefore, as a correct cipher of the Russian army, its real warlike, disposable force cannot exceed 200,000 or 250,000 men. I mean to say they cannot cross their frontiers with a larger number to assail others. And if so, Austria has her 750,000 men, Prussia her 450,000, Bavaria her 70,000, and the rest of the German Confederacy its 400,000!

1839. *April* 19.—Tchiacheff, who was strongly recommended to me by the Emperor for his intelligence, told me in confidence yesterday that his Majesty's energy of character had been signally tested during the last winter,—he had repressed no less than *four* formidable conspiracies. This is the first Russian whom I have met with that will venture to talk on such a subject. He has travelled a year or two in the United States.

At eight o'clock, expecting to meet all the Imperial family, we went to the ball at Prince Youssoupoff's. The Emperor and Grand Duke Michel attended, but the Empress excused herself by sending word that her physician advised her staying at home, and all the Grand Duchesses remained with her. The interest of the evening to me arose from the presence of Marshal Paskevitch, with whom I had several agreeable chats. He is a younger man than I had supposed, has a lively air, and is frank and agreeable in conversation. He told me he was fifty-five. His decorations, crosses, and orders were extremely brilliant, glittering on his left breast and from around his neck like a huge mass of diamonds. The Czar, after his usual kind shake of the hand, said he had not been to a party for nine weeks; that he wanted to induce his wife, whose health was bad, to stay at home by setting the example. Everybody agreed in considering the entertainment the most splendid which could be given in Europe by any person below royalty. The whole of the magnificent house was thrown open, and I have seen nothing here to surpass the elegance of the ballroom and the great supper-hall, which communicated by a columned passage, at first crowded with flowers and curtained. As two harmonious and united apartments, they are not surpassed by anything at the Winter Palace or Hermitage. They are of white mock marble; the ballroom, an immense square, with splendid pilasters, its ceiling arched and richly painted; the banqueting-room, a vast oblong, with vaulted ceiling carved in relief, and supported by twenty immense Corinthian columns of the purest and most polished white, with two galleries, one at each extremity, for music. Nothing could transcend the magic of the supper: its groves of orange-trees, towering eight or ten feet above the heads of the guests, and laden with fruit and flowers; its gorgeous arbours, prepared for the Empress, over which hung in clusters ripe, red, white, and purple, intermingled with leaves, grapes of the largest and most luscious appearance; its gorgeous and glittering table ornaments; its golden chandeliers; its dazzling company, and still more dazzling liveried servants. When from these two rooms the eye passed to the adjoining ones, to the antechambers, the refreshment saloon, the endless suite of halls and galleries devoted to paintings and sculpture, the card-rooms, and the expansive branching stone staircase, flanked with marble statues and fragrant with exotics, it was difficult to suppose the whole the creation and property of a private subject. He is said, however, to enjoy an incalculable revenue. He is, however, sufficiently noted already in the Diary. I could not help thinking that the Empress stayed away, not because of any real malady, for she walked on the English Quay this morning, but in order to avoid witnessing or countenancing a fête that approached too near the Imperial style to be agreeable in a subject. The poor Princess, who had hoped to make it worthy of her mistress and her guest, looked the picture of despair when told that she could not come.

1839. *April* 20.—The evening spent at the *soirée dansante* of Countess Schimmelpenninck. I met here most of the diplomatic chargés and secretaries, the ladies Shakoffsky, Serriavène, Paschkoff, Soltikoff, Brunoff, Pleicheyeff, Chevietz, Cavacoff, etc. Among the gentlemen were Villafranca and General Danieleffsky. I had with the last a long and interesting conversation on the condition and history of Russia, and the characters of the Emperors Alexander and Nicholas. His mind is turned closely to these subjects, and he is now actually preparing for the press a work on the campaigns and policy of the late autocrat. He accompanied Alexander as confidential secretary throughout all his great movements from the year 1804. He recently finished a portion of his history, and sent it to the Emperor for perusal. Shortly afterwards, while riding on the English Quay, he saw his Majesty walking, who made him descend from his calèche. "Savez-vous, mon cher," said he, "que votre ouvrage m'a couté bien de larmes!" He then spoke of the excellent heart and forbearing temper of his deceased brother in the tenderest manner, and declared that he had described the gentleness and wisdom of Alexander amid crosses and obstacles which would have made *him* "crever de colère." Danieleffsky looks upon Nicholas as a man of extraordinary energy and most determined purpose. "And think of such a person," exclaimed he, "avowing that he had wept over a narrative of his brother's virtues and trials! Such a monarch to talk of shedding tears!"

Among other matters, I remarked to Danieleffsky that I felt surprised at their retaining, in a country like this, the law for the equal distribution of intestate estates, abolishing primogeniture; that their aristocracy must inevitably become poor and lose their consequence; and that we regarded such a law as the very corner-stone of our republicanism. He replied simply, this is a despotism. Our Senate now merely records after attesting the Imperial ukases. Peter the Great once made an ukase establishing "les majorats," or the right of primogeniture. The nobles soon felt their independence, and in less than twelve years the Senate, while recognizing Peter's title to the throne, had advanced so far in their pretensions that they presented for his signature a written constitution of government! The law was certainly not the exclusive cause of this,—great political results require a combination of causes,—but it was the leading cause, and Peter abolished it without delay. Thus, when the object is the same, the abasement or destruction of aristocracy, a republic and a despot must pursue the same course.

1839. *May* 2.—The ice began to move downward just below the bridge this morning. It remained stationary, however, opposite the English Quay, until half-past nine in the evening, when it moved slowly, and the bridge was swung to the inland shore.

The Emperor met young Meyendorff with a companion near the Boulevards the other day. He was on horseback, they walking on foot. Having been long absent from Russia, the young men did not know the person of the sovereign, and of course omitted the customary bow. His Majesty immediately dismounted, went up to them, and reprimanded them sternly. They in vain pleaded their ignorance of his figure. He ordered them to proceed forthwith to the guard-house, and, upon their remaining stationary, not knowing where the guard-house was, he called up a sentinel, and directed him to accompany them to the prison. They were extremely alarmed, wept bitterly, and were immured for some hours in a wretched cell. At the expiration of that time, a guard announced to them that the Emperor had ordered them to be escorted to the Anischkoff Palace. They went, expecting little short of Siberia or decapitation. When at the palace, they were stationed near a corner of one of the apartments, and then left to themselves. They were surprised to notice that several young ladies now and then popped their heads in at the door, and, looking at them for an instant, retreated laughing. At last the Emperor came in, and, walking towards them, said, " Young gentlemen, you have had lesson enough for the present. I am sure that you will know me hereafter, wherever you may see me.· And now, to remove the impressions of the day, come and dine with my family and myself."

As an illustration of the extent to which the most important matters are subject here to Imperial whims, I got the following from young Count Nesselrode: The Empress, having written a letter to her father, gave it to a servant to put into the hands of a courier, then waiting to start. The servant, misunderstanding the order, deposited the letter in the post-office, and the mistake was not discovered until five or six hours had elapsed. In the meanwhile, the regular mail for Prussia, and, indeed, all Western Europe, was made up and despatched. As soon as she was told what had been done, the Empress sent an express to command the whole mail, bag and baggage, back to St. Petersburg. About fifteen hours were lost. Everything was reopened, the Imperial missive recovered and placed in the courier's care, and then, but not till then, the mail allowed to resume its journey.

1839. *May* 3.—An Imperial "*Cercle*" at noon in the Winter Palace. It was more than usually brilliant, especially in the attendance of a throng of Senators in their full dress costume of scarlet, embroidered with gold, and white underclothes. The Emperor asked me which one of the American Legation had recently gone to the United States. I told him no person; that a merchant, some four or five weeks ago, had been given a courier's pass, but no individual attached to the Legation had left it. He said somebody had told him otherwise, and he could not conceive who it was that had gone. The Empress asked particularly about Philip, whom she said she saw often on the quay. One of the family of the Austrian Esterhazys was presented. His dress was Hungarian, exceeding rich and becoming, but very fanciful.

1839. *May* 5.—A great ball and supper given by their Imperial Majesties at the Winter Palace. Mrs. Dallas and I repaired to it at half-past eight. There were said to be a thousand persons present; among others, two tinselled and ugly Queens of Georgia. With all its magnificence, it was dreadfully tedious and fatiguing.

1839. *May* 10.—For the first time this spring, we walked in the summer gardens between two and four o'clock. The alleys were crowded with fashion and rank, and among them all the ladies of the Imperial family. There is, however, not a symptom of verdure or vegetation, and the air, notwithstanding the brightness of the sun, is rather chilly. The river is free from ice at present. The Emperor has been feverish, and again leeched.

Dissatisfaction prevails in Ethonia and Livonia with some recent attempts to control and abolish certain of their ancient usages and rights. It is said to be a plan of Bloudoff, Ouvaroff, and Daschkoff, to which they gradually persuaded the Emperor to assent. A deputation from the provinces has recently been here, and was favourably received by his Majesty.

The Emperor, it is said, entertains the design of obliging all the public officers, civil as well as military, to be always dressed in their official costume. He has meditated it for some time.

1839. *May* 12.—The antic flourishes of Imperial parade made by her Majesty and her eldest daughter at the summer gardens to-day, with changes of dress and equipage, transcended the idle and ludicrous! The Emperor was ill, or I do not think he would have permitted them.

1839. *May* 27.—This being the day following Pentecost in the Russian calendar is a high holiday, and in the afternoon and evening is celebrated by immense crowds promenading to bands of music in the summer gardens. In the olden time it is said to have been customary to parade the marriageable girls of the mechanical peasants that they might be seen and be offered for as wives. There is nothing now amusing or attractive in the proceedings; the throng is mostly composed of lounging men; the peculiarities of national costume are disappearing; and as to female beauty, it would seem to be rigidly proscribed.

1839. *June* 7.—Rose this morning, after long and serious reflection, under the solemn conviction that it was my duty, at all hazards, to take my family home this summer, and, if my recall were not sent before I reached there, to abide the decision of the President whether I should return here myself or not. I accordingly inquired into the best modes of quitting, and find that my most convenient and economical course will be to proceed hence to Havre on board the steamer The Paris, on the 24th of July next. I must set about preparing for this.

1839. *June* 25.—Strange and interesting rumours are afloat. It is said that the intended wedding in the Imperial family, which was appointed for the 2d of July, will be postponed till September. Some ascribe this to the interference of the mother of Prince Leuchtenberg, who cannot consent that her grandchildren shall be all brought up to the Greek Church, as the Emperor has insisted; others ascribe it to the necessity of waiting till the great review at Borodino shall be terminated; others to the continued illness of the Empress; others to the universal repugnance manifested by the Russian nobility to the match. Most persons agree that, if once postponed for any cause, there is danger it will not take place at all. Another rumour is of political moment,—that Ibrahim Pacha is about to lead his army, in alliance with Persia, against the British Indies.

1839. *June* 27.—Agreeably to arrangement, went at half-past nine in the morning, by the railroad, to Sarsko-Selo. We had with us Madame Daschkoff and Mr. Chew. On arriving at the car-office at Sarsko, we hired five double-seated droschkies, and drove *en cavalcade* to see the gardens and their wonders. We first entered the great and older Palace. In the chapel, which was of Chinese order, rich black and gold, a mass was quietly performing by two priests for the repose of the soul of the late Grand Duke or Emperor Constantine.

The quantity of carved gilding was beyond description in all directions. I stepped off one dining- and dancing-room, ornamented at each end with shelves on shelves of ancient China vases, and found it to be one hundred and fifty feet in length. The apartment, completely covered with amber, some of it most exquisitely cut, is more curious than handsome. It was a present from Frederick of Prussia to Catherine II. The room, whose floor is worked with mother of pearl, rather disappointed expectation; but the agate room, though small, is exceedingly beautiful. The *cabinets* are all in great luxury and taste. But the most delightful portion of this vast pile is certainly the lofty colonnade erected by Catherine II., which commands the most beautiful prospects, is reached from the gardens by a gigantic stairway adorned by two huge bronze statues of Heventer and Peace, and is enriched by a succession of fine bronze busts of ancient worthies. Among the latter I detected, at a distance, the head of Fox, by Nollekens, executed in 1791, and stationed between those of Demosthenes and Cicero. At a distance was seen a pavilion on the grassy margin of a large lake, which on examination I found to contain some beautiful marbles, especially two Turkish busts, a male and female; and in another direction rose an obelisk dedicated to Sumaroff. Some fine swans are reposing near the water. On quitting this Palace, we took again to our droschkies and proceeded to what is called the large garden, into which we drove in search of various objects of notoriety and taste. The mock ruin of a château first attracted us; and we here saw the statue of Christ, of pure white Italian marble, executed by Dannecker in 1824. It was standing alone in a gloomy and desolate apartment, and seemed almost to furnish the only light we had. The drapery is a long delicate shirt, and suggests the idea that the artist intended to represent our Saviour as he rose from the sepulchre. There was something fine in the clear brightness of this tall, pure figure contrasted with the sombre-seeming desolation around it. Our next visit was to a collection of llamas, whose necks and heads struck us as remarkably graceful and spirited, the round black eye especially,— although they in general bear so near a resemblance to young camels. We thence went though numerous and beautiful windings to the antique armoury; and here we were treated with a sight of uncommon interest and splendour. The Emperor has collected a vast number of almost every description of ancient armours, particularly those of the early Sclavonians and those of the middle ages connected with chivalry, and has adapted them to figures, both on foot and on horseback, so admirably, as to represent to the eye the use and character of each perfectly. One hall has the Round Table in it, with mounted knights encircling it, in the full equipment of steel, some in the act of making battle, and others receiving the reward of valour. The immense swords, double-handed and rapiers, the richly-cut and emblazoned shields, the casque of every shape and contrivance, the enormous stirrups and rowels, the battle-axes and lances, the chain hangings, and the various trappings to protect and adorn the horses, all were in reality before us and in exquisite distinctness and truth. Several smaller halls were similarly filled with full-sized images and innumerable weapons. Here was the veritable sword of Tamerlane, one of Dmitri Ivan, one of Peter the Great, many that had been successfully employed by great Russian generals, and Turkish sabres of distinction and inconceivable richness. Hanging on the walls were instruments of chase and sport as well as of battle; and the splendidly-carved horns of many a noble huntsman are identified by their labels. We were particularly shown the spy-glass and portfolio of Napoleon taken at Moscow, the latter divided into compartments for notes or memoranda, with gilt labels of "*Légion d'Honneur*," "*Ministre de l'Intérieur*," "*Marine*," etc. In one room, carefully locked and *sealed* in glass cases, which stood upright and open to the *sight* on all sides, were the gorgeous and invaluable horse-trappings presented to the Emperor by the Sultan Mahmoud at the Treaty of Adrianople. The saddles, housings, holsters, and bridles are covered with diamonds, some of which are as large as a good-sized chestnut, and most elegantly worked in wreaths of flowers. The knobs of the pistols are huge diamonds, the handles of the swords and their scabbards are strewn with the same dazzling profusion, and the vast stirrups are of solid gold. Nothing can surpass the magnificence and beauty of these articles, truly worthy to come to such a sovereign as Nicholas from the successor of Mahomet and Saladin. We were shown a boot that had been nearly worn out by Charles XII., of Sweden, and our ears were stunned, though pleased, by a Chinese gong which was struck by our attendant. We all regretted the necessity of leaving this interesting museum, whose arrangement was so perfect and whose contents were so inestimable, without being able to give more time for a thorough examination. Our course was then directed to what is called "*The Farm*," that is the Dairy, and the residence of the cattle. The cows and bulls were superb animals,—English, Dutch, Tyrolese, and Bohemian; nothing could be fatter, fuller, more contented and more clean. They were literally living in clover, which, fresh cut, was collected in heaps, ready for their mouths. Their palaces were commodious and as fragrant as a pail of new milk; defended on one side from the sun by white curtains, and painted and kept perfectly white. One of the palaces is for their winter accommodation, closer and warmer than the other, which is open and cool. The creatures seemed to revel in sober delight with their Imperial fare, lodging, and condition, and gazed on us in all the good-humour of conscious luxury. The region of milk, cream, butter, and cheese, with its sweet atmosphere, its ice-house, its spring-house, its storehouse of various crockery, and, finally, its snug parlours prepared for the accommodation of the Imperial family whenever they thought proper to drink the beverage peculiar to the place, or to eat the sour cream much in vogue, were all inspected and admired, while we were guided by a young German woman both neat and pretty. The sheep were not at home. I inquired the way to the horses, expecting to have a view of the present stables and their glorious inhabitants, but was directed to a building of less interest; it was the stable of the "Pensioned Steeds." These were the aged and worn-out favourites of the late and present monarch: one had borne Alexander when he entered Paris, and another had carried Nicholas against the Turks; one was called Fritz, another Matilda, etc., and none were less than twenty-seven years of age. Several seemed scarcely able to stand. Great attention is paid to their food and comfort; they are walked out a certain distance every day for exercise on the green sward, but no bridle, saddle, or anything of the sort is allowed to remind them of their past vassalage. Among them was a favourite riding-horse of the Empress and a pony used by the present Grand Duke Alexander when a boy. On one side of this building, and under the shade of aloes and beeches, are erected some five or six granite tombs, each covering the remains of a dead horse, whose length and peculiarity of service, name, age, etc., are set forth as in ordinary monumental inscriptions. The man who ciceroned us among these graves spoke of their contents with a most pathetic manner and tone.

We were obliged, for want of time, and feeling the fatigue of more than six hours of exertion, to forego visiting the many other objects of curiosity with which these celebrated gardens abound. Driving off, therefore, on our return to the village we only stopped at the noble Palace in which the Imperial family usually live when at Sarsko. Although hurried and exhausted, it was impossible to restrain our exclamations of delight as we passed through this vast suite of splendid apartments. What paintings! A pyramid of flowers by Voelchens! Delicious studies by Horace Vernet! Italian pieces of the finest style! Then the furniture and its accessaries! The cabinets of the Emperor, which he has crowded with delineations of the different uniforms of his soldiery in all parts of this great camp, or has ranged on shelves and in glass cases exact models, about two feet high, of every company of his glittering cavalry, and on long tables diminutive copies of his brazen artillery and mortars, deserved a day to themselves, but we could not give them five minutes. Madame Daschkoff, who seized a chair for repose whenever our attention got irresistibly fixed, pointed out the wooden hill or smooth, inclined plane at which a maid of honour, in the act of sportively descending, had the misfortune or carelessness to strike against and completely knock over no less a personage than the autocrat himself! The columns in front of this Palace, and which form a lofty colonnade from two of its sides, struck me as uncommonly graceful and effective. We proceeded to the hotel of the railway, ordered and ate a beefsteak, which was really very good, or which our appetites made us think so, and getting into the cars at four o'clock reached home pretty considerably tired out, but indescribably gratified by our excursion.

1839. *July* 8.—Received this evening from the Master of Ceremonies three copies of the printed programme of the ceremonial of the marriage of the Grand Duchess Marie and the Duke de Leuchtenberg, and of the Court fêtes which are to follow.

We went this evening to visit Countess Laval at her country residence. While there, our coachman, in a fit of rage, beat the postilion so cruelly that his life is despaired of. I was obliged to send Mrs. Dallas and my daughters home in the carriage of Mr. Harris; and, having given the police-officer, called to the scene, permission to take the coachman into custody, I finally persuaded two of Count Borke's servants to drive me into the city, leaving directions that a physician should be procured and every attention paid to the injured postilion, who was removed to a hospital.

1839. *July* 9.—Having received our "billets d'entrée," we went this afternoon to see the "trousseau" of the Grand Duchess Marie. It is displayed in the "Salle Blanche" of the Winter Palace. The throng of visitors was immense, producing a heat and a pressure nearly insupportable. Our party got broken into detachments, and we were obliged to move along with the dense tide, without being able to see all that was exhibited, or to examine anything closely. The Court dresses, with their rich embroidered trains, were the most conspicuous objects, and were certainly very splendid. I counted in all one hundred and forty dresses, most of them exceedingly elegant, and some of them morning wrappers trimmed with lace. The four sets of jewelry were in two large glass desks. The toilet-tables and their ornaments, one of chased silver and the other highly-worked silver-gilt, were strikingly beautiful,—the former purchased as a present for his sister by the Grand Duke Alexander on his recent visit in England. Nothing could surpass the collection of furs, the Cashmere shawls, the countless bonnets, the laced and worked pocket-handkerchiefs, and all the et ceteras of a fashionable toilet. The services of porcelain and of silver and of silver gilt, each of great taste and execution, and apparently calculated for the largest scale of entertainment, formed, to my eye, the richest part of the display. Glass, in its most attractive shapes and in vast quantities, loaded several tables. The table-cloths, napkins, etc., were endless. Even the culinary apparatus was admirable. Indeed, it was impossible to imagine an article of use or ornament with which a bride should be provided that was not here in utmost perfection and in exhaustless quantity. The whole was truly imperial, and must have cost very little, if at all, short of a million of dollars.

On returning from the trousseau, we visited the immense ship of 120 guns in the new Admiralty which is about being launched. She is completely ready to glide into the water, and only waits a nod from the Emperor, who will probably add that spectacle to the others with which he proposes to signalize his daughter's marriage.

She is called The Russia, is 206 feet long, and the largest in the Russian navy, except one in the Black Sea, called The Three Saints. The iron-roofed shed under which she has been built is one of the lightest, neatest, most beautiful structures I ever beheld.

1839. *July* 10.—Count Nesselrode apprised me by note yesterday that he would receive me at his office to-day at two o'clock, and I went accordingly. I explained to him that I had my letter of recall; that I proposed going by the Tage on the 24th instant, and I wished him to have my passport prepared, for which I left him a written list of my family, and that I hoped to have my audience-of-leave as soon as the fêtes of the wedding were over. He politely assented to all this, and hoped that on my return to the United States I would be an advocate for continued friendship between the two countries. I had enumerated, among my family, Alexander, my Russian servant, who intends to accompany me; and the Count requested me to send to him the passport Alexander had obtained from the Governor of the city, that he might see that it was all right.

Count Bobrinsky called on me, and sat, inquiring about America, for a full hour. He promises to visit the United States as soon as the Grand Duchess Olga, to whom he is attached as chief Chamberlain, is married.

Received the regular diplomatic invitation to the approaching wedding and its fêtes.

1839. *July* 12.—The news from the Sublime Porte continues to agitate, as the Sultan is said to be much worse, and the conflict between the Turks and Egyptians is going on. The Russian Czar is understood to be expressly bound by treaty to aid the Turks. Count Michel Woronzow, the Governor of Odessa, and one of the most distinguished nobleman of the Empire in wealth, character, and influence, came to see me this morning, and remained, in various and interesting conversation, for more than an hour. He is remarkable for the unaffected simplicity of his manners and his intelligence on all topics. His left breast and neck were literally covered with orders, among which was conspicuous the Cross of St. George. He told me that all the great powers of Europe were in accord in the opinion that peace ought to be maintained, if possible, between Mahmoud and Mehemet Ali, but that appearances were just now very unpromising. In speaking upon the progress of human discovery and science, he remarked that the application of steam to propelling vessels through the water was, in fact, very far from being a modern idea; that he had himself read a passage in an old Spanish author, named Vilarete, in which it was as clear as language could make it, that an ingenious mechanic had undertaken the experiment before Charles V., and that, though he failed, its practicability was asserted by the historian, though he alleged that the machinery would be always liable to burst. So, also, he said, that during the reign of Louis XIV. a Frenchman was visited at an insane hospital by a celebrated English nobleman, who afterwards claimed the merit of discovering the steam-engine; that the alleged madman was so called and treated simply because he had over and over again pestered the chief of the Department of the Marine with earnest entreaties for pecuniary assistance to enable him to show how vessels could be navigated by steam; and the Count mentioned an authoress in whose works the whole of this last statement was made. The great merits, however, of Fulton were admitted as unquestionable.

1839. *July* 14.—At twelve o'clock, accompanied by Mrs. Dallas, I went to the Winter Palace, agreeably to invitations, to witness the marriage of the Grand Duchess Marie and the Prince Maximilian of Leuchtenberg. The foreign Ministers and ladies, after waiting with the general company for some time, were escorted by Count Woronzow to the chapel, and arranged on the two sides nearest the chancel, forming an alley for the Imperial cortège. We noticed that two pairs of pigeons entered at the open windows, and alighted, after flying around the dome, over the altar,—an incident that may have been accidental, but which many conceived to be the result of design. The Metropolitan and a concourse of twenty or thirty priests, robed in rich vestments of crimson thickly crossed with gold embroidery, and with mitres glittering with jewels and enamelled pictures, some bearing the sacred image, and others carrying wax lights, stationed themselves at the grand entrance to receive the Imperial party. Everybody wore their richest clothing; all the ladies having long trains, all except the diplomatic ones having the kakoshnick brilliantly studded with diamonds or otherwise ornamented. The bride wore a superb diadem of diamonds, and on the very top of her head a crown of the same description. Her train was an immense one of crimson velvet, deeply bordered with ermine. Of the religious ceremonies I could understand nothing; they were exceedingly tedious. There was an interchange of rings between the bride and groom, effected through the agency of the Metropolitan. They sipped the consecrated wine from the same golden goblet, and during a part of the proceeding—for about twenty minutes, while the Metropolitan was reading to them—golden crowns were held above the heads of the couple,—over that of the Grand Duchess by her brother the Hereditary Grand Duke Alexander, and over that of the Prince by Count Pahlen. At one time the couple were led, with their hands united, by the Metropolitan, three times round the altar. At the close of the ceremony, the groom led his bride to the Emperor, by whom he was directed to embrace her, and then followed the family felicitations and kissing. The Court choir performed the great Te Deum most effectively, and the cannon of the Fortress, aided by peals from all the huge bells of the innumerable churches, sent forth a deafening and yet exhilarating uproar. After kissing a number of the priests in succession, the Imperial circle left the Greek Chapel and went to where a temporary Roman Catholic Chapel had been constructed in some interior apartment, and the marriage ceremony was here performed again. We got home as expeditiously as we could at about four o'clock.

At eight o'clock we repaired to the "Bal Paré" at the Palace, La Salle Blanche, an apartment of extraordinary magnificence, its one hundred and twelve Corinthian columns, and the balustrade above them, with its immense chandeliers, having, since we were last in it, been most richly gilt. Here, also, all the ladies wore trains. No dancing was executed but the polonaise; there were no refreshments; and the ceremony lasted only for about two hours, the fatigues of the day being too much for the strength of the Empress. Among the remarkable costumes seen on this occasion were those of the Sultan of Kirghis, with his retinue, come to make presents to the Emperor on the marriage of his daughter, and of a Queen of Georgia. The Marquis of Anglesea, too, and his son were interesting objects.

1839. *July* 15.—We were bound to be at the Great Theatre "en gala" at eight o'clock. I was assigned by the Director a box in association with Count Rossi. The performance was a dull ballet, only relieved by one capital scene, representing a theatre crowded with spectators, before whom a danseuse was making her *début*, while we were supposed to be behind the scenes. Nothing, however, could equal the brilliancy of the *coup d'œil* presented when the whole audience rose to greet the entrance of the Imperial family into their box. The Grand Duchess Marie, as the bride, came in first, and was saluted with vociferous acclamations, then her husband, then the Empress, and, lastly, the Emperor.

I noticed yesterday during the wedding ceremonial an air of abstraction or preoccupation in his Majesty, and I find it to have been caused by the arrival of news of the death of the Sultan Mahmoud, who has by will directed his son, only eighteen years of age, to be under the guardianship of one of his sons-in-law until he attains twenty-five, and who directed the other son-in-law to be forthwith strangled. Nicholas seemed to-night to have in a measure recovered his spirits.

1839. *July* 16.—Escorted Mrs. Dallas, at two o'clock, to the Palace, where the Grand Duchess Marie received the congratulations of the ladies of the Diplomatic Corps, and subsequently those of the gentlemen. The Duke of Leuchtenberg accompanied her. We were also received by the Hereditary Grand Duke, whose travels during the last fifteen months have greatly improved his appearance and manners. He is stouter, readier, and more manly. He expressed great regret at our intended departure. At this presentation, the Marquis of Anglesea walked up to me, and said that he could no longer wait for an introduction, that he must introduce himself; and he went on to express his warm gratitude for the kind attentions which his son, a naval officer, whom he called up, had experienced on his late visit to the United States, hoping that I would be particular in mentioning to the President, whom he had personally known in England, his sense of his civilities. His son united in these sentiments, adding that the two months he had spent in America had been the happiest of his life. The Marquis is a striking figure, with white and sparse hair, erect in carriage, always in hussar uniform, and having a false leg so well made and fitted that, while he is stationary, the defect is imperceptible. He told me he was seventy-one, after I had guessed sixty-two.

At eight o'clock in the evening, we again returned to the Palace to a ball. It was crowded. The Empress and Grand Duchess Helen strongly expressed their regret at our departure, the latter with apparent and most attractive sincerity. During the evening I beat an Admiral four successive games of chess.

1839. *July* 17.—Went, *en grande tenue*, at eleven o'clock, to the new Admiralty, and witnessed the launch of the 120-gun ship, the Russia. The spectacle was very imposing,—the Empress on the water in her brilliant steamer, the Emperor and Grand Dukes in barges of twelve oars with flags flying, and a number of gig-brigs saluting. Count Woronzow, of Odessa, told me that the Warsaw was the largest vessel in the Russian navy.

1839. *July* 18.—Fête at the Palace of the Grand Duke Michel; though not so vast, more finished, elegant, and tasty than those heretofore witnessed,—a fountain in the ballroom, playing about twelve feet high, and falling into a basin crowded with flowers and golden fish; a balcony of great extent, hung with varied-coloured lamps, carpeted with crimson cloth, commanding a most beautiful lawn and distant prospect, and regaled by a noble band of music stationed under the trees. The supper was admirable, and the Grand Duchess Helen went round to her guests with unusual spirit and grace. The Empress broke away suddenly from the head of the table, and left the room; the Emperor scampered after her. The heat was intense.

1839. *July* 21.—Count Nesselrode, at the Prince of Oldenburg's last night, informed me that the Emperor would give me an audience-of-leave on Tuesday next at Peterhoff. Mrs. Dallas and her daughters and myself would take leave of the Empress at the same hour.

1839. *July* 23.—Started for Peterhoff at about six A.M. Soon after arriving, a written notification was circulated from Count Ficquelmont, purporting that the Austrian Archduke Albert would receive the Diplomatic Corps, at apartments assigned for him about five versts off, at one o'clock. I went with Mr. Chew. The ugly Prince improved in my estimation by the ease and intelligence of his manners. A handsome lunch was prepared for us, and we dined *en grande tenue* at about four o'clock. During our dinner, a tremendous storm of rain, thunder, and lightning arose, the effects of which were dreadful upon the bay, crowded as it was with all sorts of vessels in anticipation of the fêtes of the evening. Several vessels sunk, and many sail-boats were upset; some hundreds of lives were lost. We concluded that the great illuminations were marred. They were at first counter-ordered or postponed by the Emperor; but, upon the gust clearing off, fresh notice was given. I had driven with Julia, in a court droschky, round the grounds, and witnessed the immense preparations made. As soon as our dinner was over, we began our arrangements for the "bal masqué," appointed for seven o'clock; and, the court equipage drawing up at the hour, the company, having first refreshed themselves with an excellent cup of tea, proceeded to the Great Palace, headed by the Master of Ceremonies. Immediately upon my getting through the vast throng which impeded all the avenues, Count Woronzow apprised me that the Emperor was in his Cabinet to grant me an audience-of-leave. I shall ever remember this conference with pride and delight. It convinced me I had not lived in Russia without doing public service and achieving the reputation I desire.

The Emperor was cordial, kind, and full of feeling. He first addressed me, after we had shaken hands, upon my personal motives for returning to the United States. "At the moment," he said, "when we all have learned to appreciate you and your family, and when my whole court, without exception, are cherishing the best dispositions for you." I answered with the undisguised frankness due to such an inquiry from such a man; told him that my private affairs, the education of my children, and my limited resources compelled me to quit him, and that I felt deep regret at a necessity which I could not control. He again seized me by the hand, and assured me that he heard it with sincere pain and sorrow, and hoped that, if ever fortune should improve my ability, I might again visit Russia, and desired me to be sure of a hearty welcome. I told him that I derived some consolation in the reflection that I left him "au comble du bonheur;" that I could distinctly perceive in the happy marriage of his daughter a source to him of unbounded and unalloyed gratification, and that all I had had the happiness to see and hear of the Prince of Leuchtenberg satisfied me that his confidence was well founded. He received this remark with apparent delight, and grasped my hand anew and said, "I believe him to be an admirable young man, worthy of everything I am doing for him, and that he will make my child perfectly happy. You are right in thinking me at this moment as happy as a father can be." I then indulged in the trite reflection that the period of attaining such contentment was the one at which philosophy told us we should, in this unstable world, be most prepared against change and adversity. This thought seemed congenial to his mind: his countenance varied its expression from joy to melancholy, and he replied, giving it at once a special direction, "Yes, the ill health of my wife gives me much anxiety. I cannot persuade her to omit anything she deems a duty, and to refrain from exposure or fatigue. She becomes daily more feeble; and now, she insists upon going through the distractions of this fête, its intense and crowded heats and all its labours, as if her health were perfect." He then recurred to our political relations; was happy to know that between him and the United States there could exist no sentiments but those of the most friendly character, and hoped that I went away under the same impression. I told him that my attention to the subject had produced a conviction that our highest interests as a nation were identified with those of Russia. "Not only are our interests alike," said he, "but (with emphasis in his tone) our enemies are the same." We recurred freely to the fact that the political institutions of the two countries were radically and essentially different; "but," he remarked, "they tend in each to the happiness and prosperity of their respective inhabitants; and I am engaged in introducing some liberal ameliorations, particularly in the department for the administration of justice, which I hope will be attended by most salutary effects." I commented upon the necessity, however, of his having an eye to everything, and he said, *that*, under the circumstances of Russia, was a vital duty.

I handed him my letter of recall, which, he observed, he very reluctantly received, and he laid it on his desk without breaking the seal. We again shook hands, and I left him. Count Woronzow met me, in great haste, saying that the Empress was waiting to receive me. Mrs. Dallas and my two daughters had just taken leave of her. There was obvious impatience all round to commence the ceremonies or gayeties peculiar to the evening, and I went through as rapidly as was consistent with respect.

I then put off my sword, and put on my Venetian or domino, and entered the bal masqué. A more absolute jam of human beings, of all sorts, conditions, grades, forms, physiognomies, gaits, costumes, and tongues, cannot be conceived. The heat in the halls was intense. The polonaise immediately began, led off by the Sovereigns, before whom, as they advanced, turning in every zigzag direction, the compact mass gave way and opened an avenue for the brilliant train of courtiers, officers, and fashionables, almost as if by magic. On one occasion, as the glorious file came forward, I found myself screwed tight and motionless between two Kirghese Khans, some Chinese, and one or more Russian serfs, but, falling back resolutely, I caught the eye of the Emperor, who saw my predicament and effort, and exclaimed aloud in clear English, "I beg your pardon, sir!" to which I had no

AT THE COURT OF THE CZAR. 211

time for replying except by a bow of the head and a smile. Shortly afterwards, I perceived him approach Mrs. Dallas, and, with the polite inquiry, "Oserais-je vous demander pour une polonaise?" lead her, repeatedly, by the hand through the apartments. He congratulated her upon her intended visit to Paris; said it was a magnificent capital, and that many years ago he had attended one of the most beautiful balls given there: and he repeated to her the regret he felt to part with us.

A splendid supper was served apart from the crowd at about nine o'clock, and the chamberlains having arranged the parties which were to occupy the several *lignes* classified numerically, each carrying eight persons, and the number being about thirty, destined for the principal persons of the Court, we left the table, and hurried, amid some confusion and mud and wet, to the equipages. Ours was No. 3, superintended by Count and Countess Borke. All being comfortably seated, the Czar and Czarina, in the van, gave the order to proceed, and off we went for a drive of an hour through all the labyrinths of illumination and amid the finest displays of water-works I ever beheld. The scene was as wonderful as any of the creations of Aladdin's wonderful lamp. There could not have been less than five hundred thousand lights, arranged in every possible form, creating a bright day, shining in reflection from the beautiful lakes, and glistening behind cascades, extending into dazzling alleys of a quarter of a mile in length, forming obelisks of vast heights, or spanning in arches the rivulets which intersected the walks. The great "Jet d'Eau," the Samson or Hercules, with countless others in all directions, sparkled and rumbled most musically, while a host of festive frolickers, estimated by Count Borke at two hundred thousand, opened into avenues, as the cavalcade advanced, in front of the tents which were pitched for their enjoyment and accommodation within the open spaces of the gardens. Fine bands struck up at certain distances from each other; and in one of the widest and longest alleys of glowing fire, the court cortège, in order, as it were, to heighten their pleasure by seeing and saluting each other, turned round and passed repeatedly. It is, however, impossible adequately to describe the details or wonders of this extraordinary spectacle. To me and mine it was perfect enchantment, realizing and surpassing all we had read or anticipated.

We drove to our quarters about one in the morning, and, bent upon achieving our regulated plan, we hastily changed to our travelling dresses, packed up our finery, bade adieu to our friends, among whom we must ever affectionately remember the Barantes, the Hohenlohes, the Buteras, the Rossis, etc., and pushed forward for St. Petersburg. Here, however, began a fresh and exhaustless source of surprise and amusement. The entire road from Peterhoff to the capital was crowded with vehicles of every possible kind, forming three, and sometimes four, lines, and occasionally coming to a dead standstill. The droschky, the kibitka, the telega, the omnibus, the calèche, the carriage, the huge diligence were all in succession before us, and apparently without end, crowded by men, women, and children, in all sorts of motley wear, and with all the ludicrous appearances which follow fatigue after frolic. We laughed especially and heartily at the infinite variety of dozing, nodding, and drunken drivers. As our chasseur was on the box, our coachman found his way with ease and safety. We got home at four o'clock, pretty considerably exhausted, but unwilling to retire or lie down until a finishing hand was put to packing trunks and boxes for the departure at noon. The astonishing, brilliant, and interesting scene of the last twenty-four hours constitute a subject for much reflection and permanent delight.

1839. *July* 24.—We embarked in the steamer for Cronstadt, from the English Quay, at two o'clock.

HOME'S BEFORE US.

Away! away! from swelling hearts
  Our thoughts flit o'er the main;
Away! away! love fleetly darts
  Back to its nest again:
Exulting voices hymn in chorus,
We're free to fly, and home's before us!

Unmoor the bark, expand the sail,
Catch ere it droop the fav'ring gale.
The sun, himself in search of rest,
Now lights our pathway to the west.
Shake off the dust of foreign strand,
And bound we to our native land.
In vain to stay new friends implore us:
We're free to fly, and home's before us!

We've voyag'd through
The ocean blue;
Our steps have trod
On varied sod,
  And novel skies have glitter'd o'er us.
Tho' shone the sea
Sublime and free,
Tho' Briton's Isle
Could charm awhile,
And Russ and Dane
Wove friendship's chain,—
Away! away!
Love rules the day;
  We're free to fly, and home's before us!

But see! within our track advance
The sparkling lures of lovely France.
'Mid Europe's beauties, shall we fail to call
On her confess'd the siren of them all?
A wreath of glory girds her hair;
  Her eagle glance high lore discloses;
With melody she fills the air,
  And floats a grace o'er clouds of roses.
Sure we may pause, ere yet we speed along,
To taste her wisdom, fancy, fame, and song.
Think of her *Opera* and *Institute*,
  Her " *Château*" and " *Palais*,"
Her *Fanny Elssler* and her *Marshal Soult*,
  Her *Guizot* and *Molè;*
Think of her *Grand Hôtel des Invalides*,
  Her " *Boulogne*" and " *Boulevards*,"
Of dead *Napoleon* and his living deeds,
Of " *Champs*" and " *Ma'm'selle Mars;*"
Think of her " *Père-la-Chaise*" and " *Chambre des Pairs*,"
  Her " *Grisi*" and " *Cuisine*,"
Her " *Trois Glorieux*" and *glorious Thiers*,
  " *La Morgue*" and *Lamartine;*
Think of her deep *Catacombs*, so solemn!
  Her " *Mardi Gras*" and " *Bœuf*,"
" *Immortelles*" fading on the column,
  "Old *Henri*" on " *Pont-neuf!*"
Think of " *les Jardins*" (though their flowers be few)
  Crammed with savage creatures,
" *Les Barricades*" and *Louis Philippe*, who
  Courted *Abby Peters*.
Think on this galaxy! then think again,
Last, though not least, on *truffles* and *champagne!*

Away! away! Affection fond
These bright attractions looks beyond,
And sees beneath our parent skies
Love's outstretched arms and wooing eyes,
And hears soft accents in the air
Bidding us haste for rapture there.
To them! to them, may Heaven restore us!
We're free to fly, and home's before us!